D1555307

Class Enemy

Nigel Williams was born in Cheshire in 1948, educated at Highgate School and Oriel College, Oxford, and is married with three children. He is the author of TV and stage plays, and several novels, including the bestselling *Wimbledon Poisoner, They Came from SW19, East of Wimbledon* and *Scenes from a Poisoner's Life*.

WITHDRAWN

Class Enemy

NIGEL WILLIAMS

faber and faber

LONDON · BOSTON

First published in Great Britain in 1978
by Eyre Methuen Ltd
This edition published in 1995
by Faber and Faber Limited
3 Queen Square London WC1N 3AU

Photoset by Parker Typesetting Service, Leicester
Printed in England by Clays Ltd, St Ives plc

A CIP record for this book
is available from the British Library

ISBN 0-571-17474-4

2 4 6 8 10 9 7 5 3 1

To Suzan Harrison, Lynda Haddock and Susie Parsons

Introduction

I wrote *Class Enemy* in 1976, the year my eldest son was
born. Although it has been out of print in England for
some years, this very simple piece about some south
London schoolchildren has affected and pleased audiences
from Brazil to Finland. The Germans seem particularly
keen on it – perhaps because it was directed by Peter Stein
at the Schaubuhne in Berlin.

The perceptive reader will notice that almost every word
in the play is a four-letter one beginning with *f* or *c* and
one of the purposes of this introduction is to reassure
teachers who wish to put on the play in schools (it was
given a very successful production at Hackney Downs
School in east London) that I have absolutely no objection
to substituting 'frigging' for 'fucking' and 'arsehole' for
'cunt'. For some reason I have never been able to
understand, arseholes are more acceptable linguistically
than cunts. If you wish to drop the expletives altogether in
the interests of a lack of realism, feel free to do so. It is a
small-cast play with one set and, though all the characters
are male, it has been presented, with some success, with
women playing the parts.

I wrote the play when I was living in Brixton, looking
out at the tiny garden opposite our house where a group
of little West Indian kids played with dustbin lids and
sticks. I looked down at them from the desk where I was
writing and found myself wondering what their lives
would be like. I listened to my small son crying in an
upstairs room and asked myself, too, what life would be
like for him in a world that seemed to have completely
ignored the values taught to me by my father.

My father – ten years dead – was a headmaster at a north London grammar school, and one of my strongest childhood memories is the pride and passion he showed when talking about pupils whom I never knew except by name. Perhaps that is why this is a play about education and the value and importance of the search for knowledge in the most benighted and hopeless corners of the world. Although my characters eff and blind with a passion that, in Stein's production, was physically frightening, they devote some of the same passion to the quest for the thing that should be number one in all schools' agendas, coming even before parent–teacher committees, political correctness and good exam results – the search for knowledge. If that doesn't stimulate a lively debate, especially in schools where a large number of the pupils wonder what the f— they are doing there, I do not know what will.

Nigel Williams

Characters

Class Names	Real Names
Sweetheart	Sowerthwaite
Racks	Rakes
Nipper	Napier
Skylight	Skellet
Iron	Herron
Snatch	Cameron
Master	Master

Class Enemy was first performed at the Theatre Upstairs on 9 March 1978, and at the Royal Court Theatre on 4 April 1978. The cast was as follows:

Sweetheart Michael Deeks
Racks Perry Benson
Nipper Tony London
Skylight Peter-Hugo Daly
Iron Phil Daniels
Snatch Herbert Norville
Master Brian Croucher

Directed by Bill Alexander
Designed by Mary Moore

Act One

A schoolroom in south London. On stage are **Racks,
Skylight, Nipper, Sweetheart** *and* **Iron.** *All boys of around
sixteen, young men really. Racks is a thin spotty youth in
tattered school uniform, Skylight a fattish, blonde lad with
glasses and a solemn look about him, Nipper a punk
rocker, his uniform is so distorted as to be almost
unrecognisable. Sweetheart is the smartest of them, and
the prettiest, but Iron, the only one standing when the
lights go up, is not someone you would recognise as a
schoolkid at all. Very tall, wearing a leather jacket and
with a constantly aggressive, needling manner. The
classroom is a desert, huge cracks in the walls, desks
battered out of shape, and windows, if there are any
windows, shattered. Everything has been scrawled on or
broken. It is about half past two in the afternoon.*

Iron Jelly I tell yer.

Skylight Leave off.

Iron Fuckin' was. Fuckin' Jelly.

Skylight OK, OK. She was jelly. (*He seems weary of this
argument.*)

Iron We finished 'er Skylight. Fuckin' finished 'er.

Skylight Yeah?

Iron Yeah.

Pause.

You lot know nuffink. She left screamin'. I saw 'er.

Skylight Where joo see'er then clever cunt?

Iron Corrider. 'S mornin'.

Skylight OK, OK.

Iron We tore 'er apart.

Nipper Five K eh? K fer cunts.

Skylight Yore right. I ain't sayin' you ain't right.

Iron can't get the comeback he wants. He claps his hands.

Iron Desks.

Racks Leave off Iron eh? Leave off.

Iron Desks. Against yer fuckin' door.

Racks Ah leave off.

Iron Chicken?

Racks Tired.

Iron Carm on Nipper.

Nipper I'm comin'.

Iron Move *it*.

Nipper 'Oo they sendin'?

Iron Search me.

Sweetheart King-Kong.

Iron *Desks.*

They move. Slightly weary and Skylight last of all. Racks stays put. They've obviously done this before.

Sweetheart We done desks. Always fuckin' desks innit?

Iron You got ideas?

Nipper Pinch ver fuckin' chalk.

Iron Chalk. Fuckin' chalk. Ain't any chalk Nipper.

Racks No books no chalk no pencils no windows. Jus' us an' ver fuckin' desks.

Iron Carm *on*.

They've started to move the desks against the door.

Skylight Woss in store eh? I wonder. Woss in store?

Iron Fuck all's in store.

Racks Why we stay Skylight?

Skylight Sunning ter do innit.

Racks We done it vough ain't we? We bust ver winders we nicked the chalk, they never gave us no books, they're pissed off we bovver ter show up. 'S a jrag. Vey 'ave ter send someone in ter see us. Right? So why don' we take the 'int an' fuck off?

Racks We're tired.

Nipper Racks is tired. Racks is too tired ter wank.

Iron Never you mind why we stay cunt. We stay. You wanna go you go. While we're 'ere we shift ver fuckin' desks.

Skylight We know why Iron stays eh?

Iron Why's 'at?

Skylight Waitin' fer sunning to 'appen.

Iron Some fuckin' 'opes.

There is a rap on the door.

The door is open sir.

A voice outside: Oi!

Iron Simply press the handle sah.

The voice. It isn't a teacher: Open ver fuckin' door!

Iron I am afraid I cannot sir.

Again the voice: 'Ey Iron. You got ver wrong fuckin' number!

Iron Snatch!

Snatchs voice: Let us in eh?

Iron Desks lads.

Sweetheart Bleed'n 'ell.

Iron Our friend Snatch.

Sweetheart I 'fought vey nicked 'im.

Iron 'Ey Snatch!

Snatch Open ver fuckin' door!

Iron Woch yoo doin' in Ballsache 'Igh then Snatch? Why ain't you in Brixton?

Snatch No room in fuckin' Brixton. Anyway food's worse 'ere.

Iron Desks girls.

Sweetheart Am I pretty?

Iron Fuck off.

They start to move the desks. Except Racks.

'Oi. Racks.

Racks Knackered.

Iron You will be you don't move one a' them desks.

Skylight Leave off 'im Iron.

Iron St. George. An' wot a fuckin' jragon.

Skylight I said leave off of 'im. OK?

Iron decides to let this go. It amuses him maybe.

Iron Desks. Move it lads.

Finally the door is opened and **Snatch** *comes in. A very thick but amiable lad of West Indian parentage. He grins round. A bit sheepish.*

Fuckin' Snatch.

Snatch Thass it.

Iron Tell all.

Snatch Nuffink ter tell.

Iron Nuffink ter tell. Wot was she like?

Snatch 'Oo?

Iron Yore social worker.

Snatch 'Orrible.

Iron Probation Officer then?

Snatch Bloke.

Iron Fuckin' *'ell*.

Pause.

I 'ad a social worker once. Big tits. Used ter wear jeans.

Racks Fuck off Iron.

Iron No honest. Labour she was. Fuckin' more'n fuckin' Labour. Fuckin' Russian Red.

Racks An' yoo fucked 'er.

Iron 'Ow joo know?

Racks 'Cos you fucked ver girl in the off-licence an' ver girl in the canteen an' Iron you can't mention a girl wivout you fucked 'er. So I figured you fucked 'er. Anyway you told us you fucked 'er twenty times or more.

Iron Well yore right cunt. I did. I fucked 'er.

Pause.

We was in 'iss boat on Regent's Park. 'Miss –' I sez–

All 'Give us a fuck!'

Nipper An' she did. Right vere in ver boat. She took off 'er panties . . .

Sweetheart 'Er green silk panties.

Racks Parted 'er legs.

Nipper An' yoo fucked 'er all ver way back ter ver depot.

Sweetheart So 'ard yoo was twenty minutes early fer ver boat.

Snatch I missed all 'at.

Skylight Oh you missed a lot since you was gone Snatch. Our Iron's been full of 'em.

Snatch Fuckin' Iron.

Iron Tell us ver noos then cunt.

Snatch No noos.

Pause.

I come back terday. An't got much more ter tell. They said ter come dahn 'ere.

Iron Vey din't say 'oo they'd got in mind fer us by any chance?

6

Snatch Jus' ter come dahn 'ere.

Iron They're workin' on sunning nasty.

Snatch Yeh?

Iron Yeh. We broke every fuckin' git they sent us.

Snatch Fuckin' didn't.

Iron Fuckin' did. Sent us a 'ard nut. PE. Track suit. Muscles out 'ere. Big bloke. Queer I reckon. Sweet'eart stares 'im out.

Sweetheart puts on his posh look.

Sweetheart Sorry sir?

Iron Blush Blush.

Skylight Warn't a bad lad.

Sweetheart Luvly.

Iron Sent us anuvver Russian. Anuvver Red fuckin' Russian.

Nipper 'How do you feel that your environment affects you?'

Iron Ai don't know sah.

Nipper 'Do you feel that the urban environment situation leads to poverty and despair in the Inner City?'

Iron I feel that you are a cunt in glasses. ✓

Nipper laughs. Quite sycophantic.

Nipper 'Great. Great.'

Iron I feel it'd take fifteen years an' 'arf a' British Leyland 'fore yore cock so much as started the long climb upwards.

Nipper 'Oh chriffic young man.'

Iron I feel, really sah, that ve on'y fing ter do wiv you is ter fill yore arse wiv smarties an' flog you ter the Arabs.

Nipper 'Yeah. Do you feel that you are radicalised?'

Iron Fuck off!

Pause.

Snatch 'E never.

Skylight Warn't a bad lad.

Iron 'E was a cunt. Worse van a fuckin' social worker. Worse. Never even fuckin' taught us anyfing. Jus' 'urban' 'iss an' 'urban' that an' fuckin' essays abaht woch yoo done lars' Sat'day. I don' call *that* ejucation.

Skylight Woch yoo call ejucation Iron?

Iron Me. I'm ejucation. I'm an ejucation fer fuckin' anyone.

Skylight Yore in very real danger of becomin' a git.

Iron Yeh?

Skylight Yeh.

Iron An' yoo wanna watch it Skylight.

Skylight I'm watching.

Iron You watch it then. You watch it.

Snatch You two ain't changed anyway.

Iron We love each other.

Skylight We love each other.

Snatch Vat was it was it?

Skylight Nah. They sent us a bird.

Snatch *Never.*

8

Nipper Vey fuckin' did. Sent a girl.

Snatch 'Iss is no place ter send a woman.

Iron Thass wot I told 'er.

Sweetheart Competition.

Iron Fuck off.

Snatch Nice?

Iron When she come yes. When she left no.

Skylight 'E put ten years on 'er in a week.

Racks Fuckin' great she was. Fuckin' big . . .

Snatch Big what?

Racks Ah wassit matter?

Iron Yore losin' grip Racks.

Racks They was big though.

Snatch *What* was?

Iron 'Er ears. Nex' time vey discover a disease Racks, they should name it arter you.

Pause.

She was the last Snatch. She lef' vis mornin'. I saw 'er in ver corridoor. She lasted a week Snatch. No more. We tore 'er ter bits. Ovvers we may a' damaged. But 'er, Snatch, we ripped inter tiny lit'l pieces. Araldite Snatch, thass wot she needs now. An' even if vey stick 'er back nice as you like she'll be all fuckin' glue. 'Cos' vis lars' week Snatch we don ver bes' job ever. Donch yoo reckon Skylight?

Skylight You Iron. Not we. You broke 'er.

Iron Credit where credit's joo eh? Iss fat fucker fancied 'er dincher Skylight?

Skylight Never yoo mind 'oo I fancy.

Iron Secretive cunt. But we'll 'ave you ownin' up ter it. Eh? We'll 'ave you cryin' nah she's gone. Yet. Eh?

Skylight doesn't answer. Iron breaks off his needling and turns to Sweetheart. It's not that he relents, rather that he's disappointed by Skylight's refusal to come back at him in quite the way he needs.

OK Sweetheart. Go on 'an 'ave a look see. See wot vey dished up fer us terday. See wot ver Teacher's Chrainin' Collidges served up. Run along lad run along.

Sweetheart goes.

Got a ciggy Snatch?

Snatch Ten. Anyone else?

Nipper Nah.

Snatch Skylight?

Skylight I give up. But I started again. 'Ta.

Racks Vey stunt my growth.

Iron Wot growf' Racks?

Racks Vis growf' 'ere. Under me arms.

They're lighting up.

Iron I reckon 'ey might send two. Armed.

Nipper Wiv' dogs. An' Securicor.

Iron Blokes in 'elmets an' fuckin' great chruncheons. 'Terday's lesson is . . .'

Nipper One of 'em watchin' ver door.

Iron '. . . English Appreciation . . .'

Nipper Guy at ver door fingers 'is club.

Iron ''Ere is ver books.'

Nipper So get on wiv it.

Iron Vey 'frow us ver books.

Nipper An' run ter ver door.

Iron But too late! (*He grabs Nipper.*) We get vere first.

Nipper Vey schruggle.

Iron But we're too much.

Nipper 'Jus' doin' a fuckin' job.'

Iron Vey say. But *we* say –

Nipper 'Jus' doin' a fuckin' –'

Iron Fuck off! (*He's holding Nipper too tightly. Hurting him.*) You fuck off out of 'ere. You don' bring us any more books. Nex' time you come cunts you bring pretty women an' 'ard cash an' sunning ter fuckin' jrink. You piss of out of it wiv yore books. Even if you come in wiv steel plated fuckin' armour we'll ram yore fuckin' books back dahn yore fuckin' 'froat. 'Cos we don't want no books. We don' need books cunt. What we need is a ticket out of 'ere an' somewhere ter lie dahn where there ain't geezers tellin' us 'ow ter jress an' wor ter –

Nipper Leave off Iron. That 'urts.

Iron Spastic.

Skylight See Snatch? 'E got worse. One step away from the funny farm.

Snatch I woun't know 'bout vat.

Skylight Dincher Iron? Dincher take a look over a couple a' bins? Prospectin' like. Dincher? Eh?

Iron You shuch yore face. (*Slightly defensive. He's about to say something else when Sweetheart comes in.*) 'Iya schranger. Wot they got fer us then?

Sweetheart A gorilla. A stuffed gorilla. Wot sings.

Iron Carm on Sweet'eart.

Sweetheart Out inter ver corridoor I stroll. No one abaht. I go down ter ver first room. Look in – rows a' kids wiv clean faces an' 'ands folded. In front of 'em is a kind man wiv a kind face 'oldin' a piece a' chalk. Ver lars piece a' chalk left in ve Inner City School.

Iron You bin' listenin' ter teacher.

Sweetheart Ver faces of ver kids are radiant. Full of 'ope. I watch, amazed. Fuck me, I 'fink, fuck me. 'Ere am I, Sweetheart 5K, part of ver waste disposal unit of ver worst fuckin' schreet in ver wors' fuckin' section of ver gen'rally reckoned ter be 'orrible region or area an' 'ere before my eyes is twenty 'free lit'l angels gettin' on wiv ver learnin' process.

Nipper Oh *learnin'* process thass it.

Sweetheart And then I realise. It is not a class at all. It is a model of a class put in ter fool ver school inspectors. Teacher ain't movin'. Kids ain't movin'. Dummies. Ve 'ole fuckin' lot. I turn away, a tear in my eye, as, outside in ver playground, ver real kids are roastin' a noo teacher alive in Klu Klux Klan uniforms.

Iron Woss up Sweetheart?

Sweetheart Fuck all. I reckon vey're castin' lots as ter 'oo should 'ave us.

Nipper Not me not me please sir.

Iron Yes you. 5K.

Nipper Please not 5K please not 5K my wife my children my lit'l babies my lovely 'ome please not 5K sir.

Iron 5K cunt. 'Ere's a packet of Aspirin an' a poker. Now fuck off dahn vere.

Nipper Not 5K please not 5K anyfing but 5K oh my Gawd please not oh my Gawd no please. Aaaargh!

They break. A pause.

Racks Wot we gonna do while we're waitin'?

Iron Wank.

Racks I done wiv' wankin'. I really 'ave.

Iron After woch yoo doneter yore body Racks, women is out fer you. Yore bes' bet is ter get a piece a' lead pipin' an' teach it ter talk.

Racks I figure somewhere vere's iss bird. My age. Spotty as 'ell. Wankin' 'erself into an early grave. Wanked almost, *almost* as much as I 'ave. Anyway. One night there I am. Ahtside ver fish shop, lovely night moon an' all an' along she'll limp. Nasnell 'Elf glasses, buck teef an' 'er arm in a sling. Like sunnink jus' back from ver First World War. Like someone 'oo's bin gassed an' en run over by a tank. An we'll look inter each uvver's eyes an' we'll know. 'Iss chroo love.

Nipper Dad – da – da – da-a!

Iron So 'oo they sendin' lads? 'Oo's it gonna be?

Snatch Dunno.

Iron You know yore chrouble Snatch? No imagination.

Snatch Thass it.

Pause.

13

We could smash ver winders.

Iron You ain't even got the imagination ter think of an inchrestin' crime Snatch. Thass wot you done lars' time Snatch, winders. Remember? Thass why they gave yer probation on account you smashed every fuckin' winder in ver Science Labs. I mean can't you fink a' nuffink noo?

Skylight 'E's on'y chryin' ter please you Iron.

Iron Fuck off cunt.

Skylight Sorry. No. (*amused*) You fink a sunning Iron. While we're waitin'. You fink a sunnink.

Iron I know. We each give a lesson.

Nipper Do me a *favour*.

Iron We each –

Nipper Thass wot we're chryin' ter stop vose cunts doin'.

Iron We each give a lesson. Eh? Fer a laugh.

Nipper Ah carm *on*.

Skylight Nice one Iron.

Pause. Tense. The lads hadn't expected Skylight to come in on this.

Nice one. We each give a lesson. While we're waitin'.

Sweetheart An' ve ovver cunts chry an' break it up. Great.

Skylight No. 'Iss a nice idea Iron. I mean it's . . . positive innit? Eh?

Iron An' ver one 'oo gives ver best lesson. Gets a jam-jar.

Sweetheart Why don't we fuck off Iron? Why don't we just fuck off aht of it?

Iron To?

Sweetheart 'Ome.

Iron Thass why.

Nipper Fair enough.

Pause.

My ol' man jrinks cider. Ten fuckin' bottles a' cider a
night. More if vere's a match. An' when 'e's done, off ter
bed. On'y 'e wets ver fuckin' bed don' e? Can you beat it?
An' over ver years, it's worked dahn 'frough ver mattress
on ter ver carpet frough ver fuckin' floorboards an nah iss
jrippin' on ver geezer dahnstairs innit? Acid see.

Iron No fuckin' sob stories Nipper eh? 'Fought you was a
'ard case. None a' this broken 'ome shit. Eh?

Nipper 'Oo's tellin' sob stories?

Skylight I din't 'ear none.

Iron Skylight never talks abaht 'is Mum an' Dad does 'e?
Or where 'ey go at night. Closely guarded fuckin' secret
that. I reckon vere mental.

Skylight We playin'?

Racks I'm tired.

Iron Firs' time in ve 'ole 'ischry a' 5K when we done
anyfink conschructive an' Racks is tired. Firs' time in ve
'ole 'ischry a' 5K when we don anyfing ovver van smash
sunning an' Racks is tired. I ask yer.

Racks Conschructive. Thass a laugh.

Iron Wot is?

Racks You got some twisted reason a' yore own.

Iron Me? Me? Carm on Sweet'eart. Yore firs'.

Sweetheart Ah *cunt*.

Iron Carm *on*.

Sweetheart Fuckin' *'ell*.

Iron Carm *on*.

Sweetheart shambles up to the front.

Woch yoo gonna teach Sweet'eart?

Sweetheart Sex.

Racks Thass wot I wanna teach.

Iron Well yore too late aincher. Go on 'en. Off yer go.

Sweetheart puts on his posh voice.

Sweetheart Sex between a man and a woman is one of the most beautiful things there is.

Nipper Bollocks.

Sweetheart Ai'm glad you said that. I was just coming to that very point. If you lads look downward all of you, with the possible exception of Racks, will notice that you have two hairy circular things swinging between your legs. These are not there for decoration. Now. I want you to take them between your thumb and forefinger and squeeze hard.

Pause.

Suckers.

Iron Don' piss abaht.

Sweetheart Thass anuvver fing. When it stings – yore in chrouble.

Iron No messin'. You got ter be fer real . . . fer . . .

Nipper Give over Iron.

16

Iron I said no fuckin' pissin' abaht. I've 'ad that. Right? We done that. OK?

Racks I know yore game Iron.

Iron Woss my game 'en cunt?

Racks Yore out ter nail someone.

Iron Yeh?

Racks Fer real. An' it ain't Teacher.

Iron 'Oo is it then cunt?

Racks You fuckin' know 'oo it is well enough.

Skylight gets up. Curiously calm in the middle of a sudden tension.

Skylight Lissen. 'Ol Iron wants a lesson. Right? So. Woss ter stop us teachin'? You never know. We might learn sunnink.

But his calm only increases the nervousness. Racks gets up too.

Racks I go an' see if ver noo geezer's comin'.

Iron You'll join in ver fuckin' fun son.

Racks Skylight I ain't–

Skylight You do as 'e says.

Sweetheart now being teacher.

Sweetheart Wot've I got ter say abaht sex 'en?

Iron You got ter teach us sunning. Sunning we don't already know.

Sweetheart Gorilla goes into a pub an' asks fer a pint a' beer. Geezer be'ind ver bar finks – 'Seems a nice, well-behaved gorilla.' Pulls 'im a pint. Gorilla gives 'im a quid.

17

Geezer finks – 'We-ell. 'E's on'y a fuckin' gorilla won't know no diff'rent.' Gives 'im ten p. change gorilla says 'ta jrinks 'is beer fucks off aht of it. Nex' night. Same fuckin' fing. Gorilla comes in – pint a' beer, gives 'im a quid, geezer gives 'im ten p. change. Anyway. 'Fird night it 'appens again. An' 'iss time ver geezer's feelin' guilty takin' money off vis gorilla but business is business 'e pulls 'im a pint takes ver quid gives 'im ver ten p. change, an' 'en 'e leans over ver bar, friendly like, makin' up ter this gorilla. 'Funny,' 'e says, 'funny. But we don't get many gorillas in 'ere.' 'Beer at ninety p. a pint I ain't fuckin' surprised,' says the gorilla.

Pause.

Iron Woss 'at got ter do wiv sex?

Sweetheart 'S all I could fink of ter say. Joke innit.

Iron You got ter fuckin' teach us sunning cunt. Not fuckin' jokes. We're fed up a' fuckin' jokes. Thass no good. We're goin' ter *learn* summink this arternoon ain't we Skylight me ol' mate?

Skylight Thass it Iron. Learn sunnink.

Iron I can 'ardly wait.

Racks Leave off of 'im Iron.

Iron TALK cunt. TALK. Teach us sunnink. Yoo picked yore fuckin' subject now talk.

Sweetheart I'll jraw a cock.

Iron You do that son.

Sweetheart No fuckin' chalk.

Skylight 'Ere y'are Sweet'eart. Bit 'ere.

Iron is getting impatient.

Iron Move it.

Sweetheart 'Ere y'are. 'S a cock. Lesson's over.

Iron Ain't finished yet.

Nipper 'Free minutes. Got ter be 'free minutes.

Iron Five. Five minutes.

Sweetheart Ease up Iron. I could tell you all I fuckin' know in ver world in five minutes.

Iron Five fuckin' minutes cunt.

Sweetheart I jraw a cunt. (*He has drawn a cock and a cunt. Not too well.*)

Iron You ain't told us nuffing noo.

Sweetheart Sex, boys and girls, is a matter a' one a vese findin' one a' vese an' 'en 'ammerin' back an' forward like a steam 'ammer fer a couple a' minutes. Any questions?

Iron Vis still don' rung chroo ter me Sweet'eart.

Sweetheart Sex is wot 'appens when a boy bumble bee buzzes 'frough ver fields in summer an' sees a flower. When 'e sees ver flower, ver bumble bee buzzes up to it an' 'overs over it. Ven 'e fucks it rigid. Thass sex. Oh – an' birds do it an' all.

Iron You ain't chryin' Sweetheart.

Skylight 'E's chryin' Iron. Look at ver fuckin' sweat on 'im. 'E's breakin' 'is fuckin' balls. So ease up an' lissen eh?

Iron Look Bugner or wotever yoo calls yore fuckin'–

Racks Woss wiv' you two will you tell me vat? Will you leave off of each uvver? Some of us is chryin' ter get some sleep.

Iron Fuck off. You ain't chryin' Sweet'eart.

Sweetheart I tell you what sex is.

Pause.

Sex is scorin' birds innit? An' donch yoo worry 'bout me on vat score 'cos I scored plenty. I do all right. Right? I keep meself smart see. Smart. I tie ve ol' tie like thisaway. OK? Windsor innit. An' when I want I jus' crui-uise in like Jack the fuckin' lad. I got a disco 'en I? I mean you know about my fuckin' disco. 'Midnight Blue.' Well. Stands ter reason I don' 'ave no chrouble wiv gear like vat. Speakers a mile 'igh, none a' vis Sony junk I got it special from a black geezer dahn ve market. Yeah. So donch yoo worry about me an' sex boy. You better believe it. I got vat sown up son. I score when I fuckin' choose don' I? Yeah.

Only just holding himself together. Iron's got to him. Watches him, amused.

Iron Personal confessions is not on eh Nipper?

Nipper Vey may be used as a 'teachin' aid'. But vey ain't teachin'.

Iron Yoo 'ave nearly gone yore five minutes lit'l man. But owin' ter yore desire to answer fuckin' questions we never arst yer I'm afraid vat I mus' warn you vat you ain't won ver fuckin' jam-jar. An' 'till you come in wiv sunning vat ain't a joke or a nervous nelly heap a' shit yoo'll be up there son.

Skylight Iron makes ver rules a' this lesson.

Iron So wot if I do? No uvver cunts goin' ter –

Skylight Now. 'Ere we are. No teachers in sight. An' yore comin' on like a teacher. Now ain't it us 'oo makes ver rules Iron? Us. Democratic. Eh?

Nipper 'Ey Iron. Chroo you got an IQ a' 'free unjred an' twenty?

20

Iron 'Free 'unjred an' twenty five. An' 'at was before my ol' man jropped me on ver kitchen floor.

Racks Iss on'y 'is mean nacher brought 'im 'ere.

Skylight You take it away Iron. You carry on. Buch you remember. Ain't no way yore crossin' us.

Iron You ain't finished Sweet'eart!

Skylight relaxes.

'Fore yoo go you got ter teach us sunning abaht yore chosen subject. You got ter say sunning that adds up. OK?

Sweetheart Sex is . . . (*He's sweating.*) Sex is what . . . separates a man from a woman . . . iss wot vey do tergevver in . . . er . . . marriage . . . the . . . er . . . sperm go inter ver womb an' . . . birf results an'. . .

Pause.

It can be done outside marriage or inside marriage. Venereal disease is a dangerous disease. Terday vere is sex everywhere in adverts an' so on. (*He stops. Nothing more to say. But he does want to say more. He's trembling with the effort. But no words seem to be there.*)

Iron Thass yoo finished eh Sweetheart?

Sweetheart Yeah. Thass me finished.

Iron Well 'at was fuckin' useless. Facts. We don't want fuckin' facts. We want knowledge. Thass wot we come 'ere for. Not fer yoo ter tell us 'ow round ver fuckin' world is or wot 'ydrogen smells like. Knowledge Sweet'eart. Where was ver fuckin' knowledge in woch yoo said? Where was sunning ter give us a lit'l lift up eh? A lit'l 'elp eh?

Nipper I don' get any of vis.

Skylight Thass the game Nipper innit? Knowledge. Funny ol' game though innit?

Racks I ain' in vis fuckin' game. I tolj yer. Not wiv you two at it. Fuckin' Iron an' fuckin' Skylight woch yore on abaht I dunno.

Snatch I dunno woss 'appenin'. I ain't got a clue woss 'appenin'. I'm lost I am.

Iron Woss noo?

Racks You tanglin' wiv 'im Skylight? You messin' wiv 'im. Cos' yore barmy if you are.

Skylight Yeah?

Racks You don' wanna take 'im on Skylight.

Nipper Fuckin' Iron.

Snatch Wey hey.

Racks Fuckin' Iron.

Pause.

'Member ver firs' time I come across you you cunt. Fuckin' famous you was even 'en. You was over by ver sheds – by yerself. All alone. 'Oo's 'at? I sez an' someone sez 'yoo wanna watch 'im son. 'Turns out yoo 'ate ver teachers 'ate ver school 'ate ver fuckin' ground yoo walk on an' you're dangerous. An' you're fuckin' 'ot to 'andle. Stay away is ver message. Stay away. (*He gets up.*) An' now 'ere *you* are Skylight walkin' schraight in. An' yore fuckin' famous fer bein' ver ovver fing aincher? I mean yore 'alfway decent eh? I mean yore even good ter fuckface 'ere. I mean you was even good ter *me*.

Skylight 'Ow was I good ter yer Racks?

Racks Never mind 'ow you was good ter me.

22

Nipper 'E cut out page 'free a' the Sun for yer on account yore fingers shake when yoo look at it.

Racks I tell yer. Four years back –

Sweetheart Christ almighty.

Racks Four years back I'm in ver back yard wiv' two cunts from across ver way an' we're arguin' abaht foo'ball. None of us know fuck all abaht foo'ball but vere we are arguin' abaht it becos' we fink we should be an' every ovver cunt in ver place is arguin' 'bout foo'ball. Anyway. I say sunning an' one of ver cunts sez 'Racks. Fuck off.' 'Why?' I sez. 'Becos'' 'e sez 'iss well known yore a cunt.' Anyway – 'at vat moment you was passin'.

Nipper On wings.

Skylight An' wot'd I say?

Racks You said – 'I don' fink it's *well* known son. I 'fink we're chryin' ter keep it a closely guarded secret.'

Skylight Geddaway.

Racks Thass it.

Skylight An' 'ass why yoo foller me roun'?

Racks Oh I quit follerin' you Skylight.

Skylight An' thass 'ow I was good ter you eh?

Racks Thass it.

Skylight Fuckin' 'ell Racks. Woss it like when someone's nasty to yer?

Sweetheart They pinch 'is 'anky.

Racks Vey don' say nuffink. Vey pass me in ver schreet an' 'ey don' say nuffink. Vey look 'frough me. Vey don' even

23

'ave ter look 'frough me 'cos I ain't 'ere. I'm dead. I'm
dead an' on ver moon. I'm a fuckin' ghost. I'm Racks ver
Wanker, so fuckin' empty 'e might be a genius. Oh. An'
mos' people do.

Skylight Do what?

Racks Ignore me.

Skylight Nah's yer chance Racks. Teach us sunning.

Racks I ain't –

Skylight Teach us.

Nipper Fer uncle eh?

Iron Aaah. Glad ter see yore chippin' in Skylight. Glad ter
see yore keepin' yore lad up ter mark. Glad ter see yoo
want us ter get on wiv' vis lesson nice an' peaceful.
(*suddenly vicious*) Nah. You get up on yore 'indlegs cunt
an' yoo make a positive conchribution or yoo won' know
wot 'ich yer.

Racks I'll fish it aht.

Iron I said a *positive* conchribution Racks. Chalk.

Racks Gordon bleed'n Bennet. (*He gets up, yawns.*)
Knackered.

Iron Woss it ter be Racks?

Snatch 'Ey. Racks give a lesson. 'Ow about it eh?

Skylight Carm on son . . .

Racks Gardenin'.

Iron *Gardenin'*? *Gardenin'*? 'Ave yoo lost yore marbles
son? Gardenin'? Where ver fuck yoo fink yoo are?
Petworf'? You turnin' inter Percy fuckin' 'Frower? Vis is
Ballsache 'Igh son ver land God forgot an' town planners

24

do not remember. The 'ole son. The black 'ole a' London.
Woss gardenin' got ter offer us?

Nipper More'n sex anyway.

Sweetheart Sex and gardenin'. Now there's a thing.

Racks Gardenin'. I wanna teach abaht gardenin'.

Skylight Well. Teach.

Racks Steady Skylight.

*He is going out front. Slowly. He turns, suddenly being the
teacher. They fall quiet.*

Winder boxes.

Iron 'Ooray.

Racks 'Winder boxes make a nice addition to the flat or
home. You would be surprised, friend, how you can
transform your environment. Are you fond of keepin'
busy? Of an evenin' resist the temptation to 'ang around
outside of yer pub wiv' a couple a' broken bottles waitin'
fer an' ol' lady ter pass by. Why not, jus' this once, avoid
yer dreary ol' business of bashin' 'frough car winders an'
nickin' 'em. Even, I say, give up writin' yore name on walls
wiv' WANKERS nex' to it in big, red letters. 'Fink big by
finkin' small.

They're listening.

First of all – buy yore winder box.'

Nipper Where?

Racks Gardenin' shop. Or make one.

Nipper *Make* one? You barmy?

Racks My ol' man makes 'em isself.

Sweetheart Wot a cunt.

Snatch Thass difficult.

Racks Few bits a' plywood – bit a' paint. Joint 'em if yer want ter.

Iron I 'fought vis was gardenin' not woodwork.

Skylight Leave off of him.

Nipper Christ almighty. Vis is worse than 'avin' a teacher.

Skylight Yeh?

Nipper We be pullin' 'im ter bits in a moment eh Iron? Jus' like yore girl teacher Skylight eh?

Skylight You reckon Nipper?

Pause.

I don't son. I tell yoo wot I reckon abaht yoo. You're fuckin' cannon fodder thass woch yoo are. I woun't chrust yoo wiv' walkin' in front a' me wiv' a rhino gun. You're wot vey say we are Nipper. Yore fuckin' scum yoo are son.

Nipper My turn's comin' cunt. Jus' wait. Jus' yoo wait.

Sweetheart 'Ey boys an' girls I got a–

Racks Please people! Please!

A silence.

I wuz tellin' yoo abaht ve art an' craft of makin' an' employin' winderboxes. Ve ancient an' honourable art of fuckin' abaht wiv' bits a' wood an' ve odd packet a' seeds from Woolies. Now. 'Avin' maj yore box yoo piss off out of it an' obtain some soil.

Nipper Soil? Soil? Where you gonna get soil?

Iron Speak friend.

Nipper Cunt. Where's 'e gonna get soil? Eh? You tell me. Vere ain't any soil round 'ere.

Racks Yoo go into a garden shop. Or inter ver countryside. An' yoo pick up a 'andful. An' yoo shove it in ver box. An' 'en yoo buy a packet a' seeds. An add water. An' in ver Spring, one Spring mornin' you go ter ver winder ter watch ve ambulances go past or ter check up 'oo's bin stabbed on ver pavement dahn below an' lo! A geranium. A hydrangea. A lily. A rose. A lit'l flower peepin' up ach yer makin' it firs' bow in ver big wide cruel world a' SW 329. 'Hullo lit'l flower!' you say. An' suddenly yore day is chransformed. Nacher 'as raised 'er 'ead, spreadin' 'er lit'l 'and all rahnd yer an' yoo realise vat all is not in vain. So – ver launjrette's closed. So – ver chube's fucked. So – you got done over, or belted lars' night. But still – in yore winderbox is a fuckin' geranium. It ain't all bad. Eh?

Nipper Wot a wanker!

Iron I mus' admit Racks . . . that so far . . . yoo are failin' ter convince me.

Nipper See. Cunt. Like Iron sez yore –

Iron Fuck off.

Pause.

So far, Racks, I feel a lack.

Sweetheart Wot we s'pose ter do wiv' 'iss geranium anyway?

Skylight Look at it.

Racks Look at it.

Iron *Look* at it! *Look* at it! You barmy? Wot use is lookin' at a fuckin' geranium?

Skylight 'Oo said anyfing abaht use?

Nipper Fuckin' winderboxes. Make yer puke.

Iron Fuck off Nipper.

Nipper Leave off of us Iron I –

Racks My ol' man –

Sweetheart Da – da – da-a!

Racks My ol' man. 'E lives off of Clapham Road. One room. My ol' lady fucked off wiv' a geezer from Raynes Park. Right? Anyway. There 'e is. One fuckin' room over a terbaccinist. Vere 'e sits. Wiv' vis winderbox 'e made 'imself. Nah. After 'e'd made it, see, 'e shoved it aht on ver windersill, wiv its soil an' its seeds ver lot. Regular lit'l garden. What 'appened? Cats got it. Cats peed on it, shat in it, fucked in it, sang in it, danced in it, staged fuckin' Grand Op'ras in it ev'ry night. Time 'ey was 'frough wiv my ol' man's winderbox it looked like a main drain. Was 'e dahn'earted? Nah. 'E went aht an' bought anuvver one.

Pause.

Filled it full of earf', shoved in 'is seeds put it aht on 'er windersill. On'y this time 'e boxed clever. 'Iss time 'e shoved barbed wire all over it. Barbed wire an' 'e odd bit a' glass an' God knows wot. Vis geranium was vee mos' closely guarded geranium in ve ol' 'ischry a' London. So wot 'appened? Cats, I dunno 'ow, but ver cats, get in. 'Ey must a' bin wearin' protective clothing but vey got inside ver barbed wire an' peed an' shat an' 'ad fullscale orgies in ver manner a' cats ver wide world over. But was my ol' man dahn'earted? Never. 'E put a fuckin' great glass bowl over ver barbed wire an' ver bits a broken glass, an' on *top* a' ver bowl 'e put a brick so ver cats couldn't lever veir lit'l paws under it an' tip it over. An' if yoo go pars' my ol' man's place (an' I don' advise it) an' look up to 'is

windersill you'll see vis fing. Like a fuckin' bunker. Like a
tank cemetery. An', somewhere, at the bottom, miles
down, light years away, un-fuckin' seeable-touchable-
smellable or get-at-able is 'is geranium.

Pause.

Thass 'is garden innit.

Iron Fuck me.

Skylight Why don' 'e do in ver cats?

Racks Animal lover.

Snatch 'Oi oi!

Iron Wot a cunt! (*Goes to him.*) You call vis knowledge
Racks? Vis is ver rocky road ter ruin yore sellin' us Racks.
Vis is worse 'an 'at bollocks abaht ve Inner City School. I
mean vis is worse 'an 'at bird ol' Skylight wet 'is knickers
over wiv' 'er greasy 'air an' 'er –

Skylight Shut up abaht 'er Iron!

Iron Well I don' like it son! (*Staying close to Racks,
ignoring Skylight.*) I know yore ol' man's sort Racks. We
got 'em in our schreet. Fer some fuckin' reason some cunt
said ver Queen was comin' dahn our schreet Jubilee week.
She was comin' dahn our schreet. 'Our street?' vey said,
'but there's shit everywhere. Woss she goin' ter fink of all
this?' NO worries they said apparently ver Queen was jus'
dyin' ter fix 'er peepers on Streatham Souf' Peckham an'
ve Empress a' slums 'erself bein' a schreet some yards ter
ver West a the establishment where we are now listenin'
ter young Racks moan on abaht gardenin'. Wild 'orses,
vey said, woun't drag 'er 'an Prince Philip away from ver
pile a' rubble, dustbins, crap of all sorts an' broken
bottles a' British Wine, that go ter make up my road. 'She
wanted,' and I quote, 'ter see it for 'erself.' (*He's got what*

he wanted: the attention of the class.) Oh she saw it fer 'erself Racks. She come 'frough at ninety miles an' hour in 'er Rolls, grinnin' like she was clockwork. An' joo know wot vose cunts done? Yoo know wot ver creeps like yore ol' man done in 'er honour? Vey fuckin' tidied it! Vey put up Union Jacks an' White Paint an' pictures a' the lady 'erself an' Prince Philip an' Prince Charles lookin' like 'e 'ad a dinin' room suite shoved up 'is arse an' it made me sick.

Skylight So pride in woch yoo do's a waste a' time is it?

Racks Yeh. Is it a waste a' time ter –

Iron Donch yoo 'pride in woch yoo do 'ter me son. I ain't talkin abaht pride in woch yoo do. I'm talkin' abaht lipstick cunt. I'm talkin' abaht people 'oo won't see wot they bin given. I'm talkin' abaht my ol' lady 'oo appens ter be an' ugly old cunt on'y she can't see it. So wos she do? Dolls 'erself up don't she? An' I see 'er in ver pub an' I –

Pause.

Union Jacks. Don' gimme Union Jacks. Two million fuckin' Union Jacks won' 'ide ver smell.

Skylight Wot a fuss ter make abaht a flag. Anyone'd fink you were fond a' flags way you go on abaht 'em.

Nipper I like a flag. Skull an' Crossbones thass me.

Skylight I know yore flag Nipper.

Nipper Woss my flag then?

Skylight Two toe-rags stuck tergevver wiv' sellotape. An' 'Vote fer Nipper' on it.

Iron Do you mind? Racks an' me was 'avin' a lit'l talk.

Racks Was we? I never noticed.

Snatch 'Oi 'oi!

Iron We do not like yore lesson Racks. This is chroo.

Skylight 'Oo's 'we'?

Iron Well it ain't you, you fat git.

Racks has broken from Iron.

Racks Well ain' anyone goin' ter take a garden? No one? None a' yer? I mean 'fink abaht it. In ver winter when ver snow jrifts up Acre Lane an' ver lit'l sparrers is 'angin' arahn ve entrance ter Clapham Norf' Tube Station tell me vis – will none a' you take a garden? Ver snow'll lie deep an' crisp on yore winderbox. All fifteen square inches of it. Fink a' Spring when yore buds is buddin' or a' Summer when all is a blaze a' glory or a' autumn when fings start to look groggy an' keel over. Consider the changin' seasons.

Pause.

An' consider my ol' man nah she's fucked off wiv' on'y a winderbox wot won't work an' a suit 'e got from a jumble sale an' me an' 'im lookin' at each uvver an' 'finkin' 'Well then. Fuck me. Well then.' (*drying up; in danger of betraying some feeling*) Fuck me.

Iron 'E'll be cryin' any minute.

Racks Shut up Iron.

Iron Feelin' sorry fer yerself Racks?

Racks I'm done anyway.

Iron Anyone'd fink this was Ancient Greece the way yore carryin' on.

Skylight Leave off of 'im.

Iron Woss up wiv' you Racks? Somebody nick yore Teddy?

Racks Scrub it Iron.

Iron It ain't that bad Racks. Is it? Iss on'y Brixton. It ain't fuckin' Gallipoli. I mean vere's geezers all over the world 'avin' their legs pulled off wiv' tweezers an' 'ere's you lookin' like death on account your ol' man's 'avin' problems wiv' 'is winderbox.

Skylight Ainchyoo never 'eard a' feelin's Iron? Eh?

Iron Feelin's fer wot? Eh? Answer me that. Teach me that.

Skylight You don' teach that Iron. You feel or you don't. Simple as that.

Nipper I feel. I feel sunning long and thin.

Iron An' I don't. Right? Is that it? I don't feel nuffing. Is that the one?

Skylight 'Ass ver way 'iss goin'.

Iron Well maybe not like you I don't. I ain't made a' rubber. 'Fank Gawd someone rahnd 'ere ain't made a' rubber.

Skylight Ah fuck off.

Nipper Rubber goods.

Skylight Yeh. Yore rubber goods aincher Nipper? You wanna watch it or I could eat you fer breakfast.

Nipper Yeh?

Iron 'E could an' all Nipper. Thass 'ow it is.

Sweetheart I can do Racks Nipper can do me Skylight can do Nipper and Iron can do ver lot of us. That right?

Snatch Wot abaht me?

Sweetheart You can't do no one Snatch. On account yore too schoopid.

Snatch 'Oo's schoopid?

Iron You done Racks?

Racks Yeh. I'm done.

Pause.

I like gardenin'. Sorry.

Skylight When she fuck off Racks?

Racks Two year ago. Sent me a letter said it was chroo love. I arst yer. Chroo love at sixty. Not on.

Sweetheart Chroo love an' a lot a' wrinkles.

Iron Well Racks. You ain't won ver jam-jar.

Racks Wot'd I do wiv' a jam-jar?

All Wank in it!

Iron But on we go.

Racks goes back to his seat. Iron once again out in front. The ring-master.

Iron Onward an' upward we go friends. 'Ow twisted is ver path ter knowledge! 'Ow it bends. ''Ere we are!' we may exclaim, at a bend in the road, 'we 'ave arrived. 'Iss is it.' An' 'en wot 'appens? The mist descends. An' so as we 'appy band a' bruvvers search for knowledge 'ere terday, 'ammer our way ter the troof – 'oo knows? Maybe it is the search that matters. Maybe ver quest is all. One 'fing 'owever, is certain – (*Sudden transition from the heavily facetious to the vicious: he turns on Racks.*) We ain't goin' ter get nowhere dribblin' on abaht gardenin'. OK?

Nipper Too right.

Iron Too right.

Nipper 'Ass ver one.

Iron Couldn't agree more.

Nipper Right. (*vaguely aware he's being sent up*) OK.

Iron Nipper. Yore on.

Skylight Yore on.

Snatch Nipper's on.

Racks Nipper's go.

Sweetheart 'Old it! Pigs!

Racks Teachah!!

Nipper 'Fank Gawd fer vat!

Iron DE-esks!

Sweetheart Too late.

Enter a **Master***. The noise stops.*

Master Which one of you is Cameron?

Nipper Me sir.

Sweetheart Me sir.

Master Come on. Which one is Cameron?

Snatch I am.

Master Sir.

Snatch Sir.

Master They want you.

Snatch 'Oo do?

Master *I* don't know. It's about some windows apparently.

Iron Oh *no*!

34

Master You better come.

Iron 'Elp us all!

Snatch I done 'em on me way up 'ere. From ver law.

Skylight Never resist a winder eh Snatch?

Snatch Never.

Master Come on.

Skylight Sir –

Master Uh?

Skylight When are they comin'?

Master Who?

Skylight 'Oo's comin' ter teach us.

Master I haven't the faintest idea.

Sweetheart 'Ey –

Master I beg your pardon?

Sweetheart Vere'll be someone. Won't there?

Master I really haven't the faintest idea.

Sweetheart Look. We bin –

Master Cameron!

Snatch Yeah.

Pause.

Yeah.

Sweetheart I mean they ain't gonna –

Master Come on.

Snatch I see you lads.

Iron Maybe you will. And maybe you won't.

Snatch and the Master go. Sweetheart watches them from the door. Then turns back. He sounds worried.

Sweetheart 'Ey. They ain't gonna leave us 'ere ter die are they?

Skylight 'Course vey ain't.

Iron 'Ow joo know?

Skylight 'Cos I know. Vere teachers ain't they? 'Ass their job. Ter look after us.

Iron They can't look after us though can they?

Sweetheart I mean it ain't –

Skylight They can keep chryin'.

Iron Well well well. Thass woch yoo reckon is it? 'Unjreds an' unjreds a' teachers like your bird wiv' greasy 'air floggin' veir way dahn 'ere ter give us ver word a' God. Don' gimme that. 'Ow many times you reckon they're gonna bovver beatin' their way dahn ter 5K? You mus' be barmy.

Skylight 'Oo's barmy.

Iron 'Iss is *it*. Now. This afternoon. This is it. You wait fer someone ter come an' teach you son yore gonna wait an awful long time. They don wiv' teachin' us. All thassover. Vey worked aht that if they leave us 'ere long enough we're all goin' ter piss off an' join the Army. Donch yoo lads run away wiv' any uvver idea. 'Iss just us.

Sweetheart Surely they'd send someone. Eh? Doncher 'fink? I dunno. If they don't iss not – (*He sounds scared.*)

Skylight 'Course vey'll send someone.

Sweetheart If –

Iron They ain't! Don' kijyerselves! (*half enjoying it*) Even ✓
lit'l girls wiv' greasy 'air an' a mouthful a' Marx. They
done away wiv' all of 'em.

Skylight Lissen Iron. No one in this world jus' leaves
people like that. I mean some might. Yoo might I don'
know. But not all. Thass all there is to it. So donch yoo
give 'em that 'eap a' shit abaht no one comin'. 'Iss
someone's job ter come even if it ain' someone's wish.

Iron Someone's job. Don' gimme someone's job. They
done away wiv jobs. Dinch yoo see it in ver papers?

Nipper Thass ver blacks done that.

Iron Ah. An idea. A view of the world. Beats gardenin' an'
sex dunnit? An idea.

Nipper Blacks done it. Well known.

Iron 'Oo by cunt?

Nipper Everyone. Iss why we're in ver shit. On account of
ver blacks.

Iron This sounds inchrestin'. A 'feory. 'Oo knows we
might even learn sunning from friend Nipper. 'Ver Blacks
Done It.' Vis mus' be right. Vis mus' be why we're stuck in
Ballsache 'Igh on a wet 'Fursday waitin' fer someone ter
come an' 'frow us a bone. 'Ver Blacks Done It.' Nice one
Nipper. Vis sounds a subject fer a lesson. Take it away son.

Nipper I ain't givin' no lesson Iron.

Iron You fuckin' are son. You are raisin' ve 'ole tone a' the
debate. I do not get the impression thach yoo are goin' ter
jroop abaht fer ten minutes on account a' yore ol' man's
lack a' talent fer gardenin'. Nor do I think you will
stammer out a few 'alf trooves abaht sex. No. I 'fink you
are gettin' dahn ter the nitty gritty, the queschion we all
wanner answer i.e. Why Are We 'Ere An' 'Oo's Fault Is It?

37

I mean Nipper – why ain't we in the Ba'amas. Or Monte Carlo. Or ver fuckin' 'Ilton. Why ain't we wiv' Prince Andrew in ver far Norf' a Canada? Why are we stuck in 'iss garbage 'ere? It mus' be *someone's* fault. I mean it can't jus' be ver luck a' the jraw can it now? So you tell us all abaht it Nipper. You tell us 'ow the Blacks Done It.

Skylight 'E's bin talkin' ter them cunts at the gate.

Racks National Fuckin' Front.

Iron Lovely lads. Woss wrong wiv' a bit a levver? You lads is way be'ind ver times. Nipper's up to all vat aincher Nipper? 'E makes Punk Rock look like Old Time Dancing. Teach us Nipper. Tell us the noos.

Nipper I ain't givin' no lesson.

Iron You fuckin' are cunt. You fuckin' are goin' ter give us a lesson. You are goin' ter give us a lesson called The Blacks Done It. An' yore gonna give us it now.

Nipper No I ain't.

Iron Yer fuckin' are!

Nipper I fuckin' ain't!

Iron Yes you fuckin are! (*Iron has him by the collar. And Iron's a strong lad.*)

Nipper OK. I fuckin' am. (*He gets up.*) You arst fer it.

Iron We did Nipper. We pleaded for it. We 'ad ter fuckin' schrangle you for it.

Nipper Favours I done you Iron.

Iron No one done me no favours Nipper an' donch yoo ferget it. No one in this wide world done me no favours right? Right. Now piss of up there an' give us some knowledge.

Skylight Wot is this bollocks anyway? 'Oo sez blacks done it? Blacks is people ain't they? Woss different? You –

Iron Oh Nipper don' mean it personal do yer Nipper? It ain't Snatch. Iss blacks in gen'ral innit Nipper? Imaginary blacks – wot live under ver floorboards. Yore diff'rent. On account yore 'ere wiv us.

Nipper I ain't sayin' anyfing against Snatch. But you tell me. Woss wrong wiv' Brixton? Woss wrong wiv' 'arf a' Souf' London? You tell me. Well known. 'Ow come nuffink works an' ver buses don' run on time? 'Ow come we ain't got no jobs an' when we piss off out of 'ere iss the schreet fer us? 'Ow come my ol' lady carn afford meat no more?

Skylight Oh do me a favour. 'Cos ver blacks are buyin' it I s'pose.

Iron 'Ear 'im out.

Nipper Ver Blacks come over 'ere 'an pinch our jobs. You look round. Vey're everywhere. Now I see 'em. Effra Road I see 'em Railton Road I see 'em up Electric Avenue an' by Brockwell Park I see 'em. Like ants. 'Ittin' white ladies over ve 'ead. All we got ter do vis geezer on the gate said is rip 'em up now affore they get us.

Skylight Starting wiv' Snatch I suppose.

Iron Carry on Nipper. Do.

Pause.

Nipper Thass it.

Iron Thass it? Thass it?

Nipper Yer.

Iron Thass the 'ow the why an' the wherefore of 'ow the Blacks done it.

39

Nipper Yer.

Iron Well thass *pathetic* Nipper. Now I ain't like this lot. I don' start prejudiced. Me in search a' knowledge. I don' say Blacks done it I don' say Blacks din't do it. All I say is 'someone done it.' Thass my position. An' if you can show me good an' sufficient reason why Blacks done it I'll be out there wiv' my levver 'at an' my big black boots burnin' men women an' childjren ter get a lit'l bit a peace an' quiet.

Skylight Filf'. Yore talkin' filf'.

Iron Can we 'ave some order 'ere! (*He silences them. As he usually can.*) Nipper 'as rights. 'E 'as rights. Nah thass democratic. Innit Skylight? Or are you scared 'e'll convince yer? Let the lad talk. Facts. Figures. Less give 'im a chance. I mean 'e's obviously bin 'finkin' abaht vis fer a long time. Yore gonna teach us aincher Nipper? Eh?

Nipper I don' 'ave ter teach yer. Jus' use yer fuckin' eyes.

Iron You fuckin' teach me cunt! (*Slaps him across the face.*) Tell me all abaht it!

Nipper I'm tellin' yer!

Pause.

Vey come from Africa mainly. Vey stowaway. On boats, planes, you name it they stowaway on it. Under planks, in boxes, in lit'l 'oles. Sometimes they 'old on ter ve underside a' ships an' 'old vier breaf' fer long periods. Sometimes ve ol' load a' them club tergevver ter buy a boat an' set aht from India or Wugga Wugga land or wherever vey live. 'Fore vey come vey 'ave a ceremony. Vey dance rahnd a pitcher a' the Queen an' 'ey pee on it. Then they take aht the British Passports giv'n to 'em by the Labour an' wave 'em rahnd their 'eads shoutin' abusive words. 'Ow they come 'ere's a closely guarded secret.

40

Always land under cover a' darkness. You can tell ver places vey land on account the beach looks kind a' rumpled. Then they 'itch a lift ter London. By minor roads. In disguise often. When they get ter London vey go schraight ter the Foreign Office ter see their black mates an' their black mates fix 'em up wiv' places on the black market – iss called that on account iss run by blacks. Oh they pay a lot fer the 'ouses. 'Firty 'fousand quid fer a two room flat in Wandsworf' which is why all of us bin on the waitin' list ten years. Once they got one flat in a schreet vey send the gang in – thass a gang a' them. They go into all the uvver 'ouses in the schreet an' cut the white people's throats an' boot 'em out the window. Then they go an' get special furniture an' stereos the size a' Buicks. After that – every 'ouse in the schreet is painted yellow.

Pause.

Nex' mornin' ver children arrive. Nah blacks don' breed like ordinary people – their children jus' pop aht a' them, schrung tergevver like sausages squeakin' like pigs. They grow in a matter a days. Like golliwogs they grow – all got up like they was in a toyshop. An' when they're done they go a-muggin'. Muggin' is like sex on'y worse. It's done to old ladies after dark and after it's bin done ter them ve ol' ladies never are the same again apparently. It's on ve increase due to Asians too. After they gone a-muggin' ver children come back ter ver fam'ly 'ome an' ey all sit rahnd sharin' out the goods. Then they all go out ter find a white woman an' rape 'er ter chrissen the noo 'ome. She 'as ter be a virgin uvverwise they don' reckon they've arrived. All the white people start ter move out an' lose their jobs but there ain't nuffink they can do on account ver Labour Government's bin took over by vese blacks 'oo leave ver rubbish in our street an' dig 'oles in our back gardens an' break up our parent's marriages an' cause chraffic jams an' foul up ver phones an' ruin ve economy. (*defiant*) Donch

41

yoo tell me that ain't 'ow ver blacks done it 'cos far as I'm
concerned thass 'ow they done it. Donch yoo tell me it
don' make no sense. It ain't supposed ter make sense. Not
like that. But you tell me whevver anyfing makes sense.
Nuffing ever made sense ter me since I was fourteen since I
was ten since I was eight since I was six since I was knee
'igh to a fuckin' lamp-post. Nuffing ever made sense ter me
so why should I make sense fer any a' you. Up you I say
when it comes ter that.

Pause.

When I was ten I wanted a pair a' long chrousers. Fuckin'
'ell. I wanted a pair a' long chrousers like nuffink on earf'.
You could a' given me a playground a' my own. You could
a' given me sweets ver lot I warn inchrested. Wot I fuckin'
wanted was a pair a' long chrousers. An' would my ol'
man gimme a pair? Wou'd 'e 'eck. No chance. I said to 'er
my tenf' birf'day 'Ma – vere ain' anuvver kid on ver
fuckin' schreet wearin' short chrousers. Ma – I look like
one a'ver Royal Family. Ma – I said – I look a cunt in vese
chrousers.' 'Son,' she says, 'since yore ol' man died we
ain't got ver money ter worry abaht long chrousers.'
Right, I 'fought.' Fuck *you* I 'fought.

Pause.

Same wiv' Prentice. Vat geezer in ver first form. 'E seen me
ver firs' day in – 'woss yore name son?' 'e says. 'Napier,' I
says, 'but vey call me Nipper on account I'm a dwarf.' E
says – 'Relax Nipper you ain't a dwarf. Yore more a rough
sketch of a dwarf, a draft-midget as it were.' 'Ow we
laughed, 'ow the joke was on Nipper fer 'avin' brought up
ver subject of 'is 'eight. But I 'fought ter meself 'Fuck you
Prentice.' Fuck Prentice and my Ma an' my Dad fer dyin'.
Fuck cats, dogs, mice, insects, bus jrivers 'cos none a' you
ever liked me. None a' you. An' fuck you. An' thass why
the blacks done it.

(*To Iron*) I wanted ter be like you Iron. I wanted ter be cuttin' 'frough 'fings. Not-give-a-damn I wanted ter be. Screw ver lot a yer. Some outlaw I turned out ter be eh? Some fuckin' outlaw. No frien's no enemies. I mean you lot you don' even like me do yer?

No answer.

Do yer? Well then. Chry an' tell me the blacks ain' in it too.

Iron Nipper you got a long way ter go. Iron ain' jus' not-give-a-damn. Oh no. Lot more'n 'at. I go where I want Nipper. You wait fer my lesson. An' it won' be no Blacks Done It crap. You win no prizes.

Sweetheart Vere's a geezer comin'. I can see 'im. Ovver side a' the block. 'Vis corridoor. 'E's comin' this way no question.

Skylight Maybe our boy.

Sweetheart Big bloke. Good lookin'.

Racks 'E really comin'?

Sweetheart This way no question.

Skylight Could be lucky. Don't bank on it but could be.

Racks Woss 'e wearin'?

Sweetheart Blue shirt. Sports jacket. Glasses. Big though.

Skylight 'E carryin' books?

Sweetheart Few books.

Skylight We may be in luck.

Sweetheart See fer yerself.

Skylight Safer from 'ere.

But Sweetheart stays by the door. Excited.

Sweetheart 'E's comin'. Inter the Science Block. Christ 'e's big though. Swingin' 'is fuckin' arms. 'E's got blonde 'air. 'E's stopped. No. 'E's comin' this way yeah 'e's comin' this way I can see them books Skylight no 'e's comin' this way. 'E's young though I mean 'e's twenny five-six no more. 'E's noo. 'E's got ter be noo. Can't be worse eh? Van ve ovvers? Eh? Oh come *on* son.

Pause.

Iron We won't need no teacher. Not till we finished the lesson.

Pause.

Sweetheart An' now 'e's lookin'. Seen me. 'E's jus' startin'. Lookin' schraight at me. 'Ey this is weird. Noo. Definitely noo. Well don' jus' stand there son. I mean 'e's close lads. Forward or backward march eh? 'Ey Mister. Come on then. Move this way if you would be so good. Please. *Please.*

Pause.

Iron Like I said. Not till we finish the lesson.

Slow fade.

Act Two

Exactly where we left them in Act One. Sweetheart is still at the door. The others turned away from him apart from Skylight, who seems the only one interested.

Skylight 'E ain't moved?

Sweetheart Stood still 'en 'e?

Skylight So call.

Racks Yeh. You call to 'im cunt.

Sweetheart Mister! 'Oi Mister!

Skylight 'E move?

Sweetheart 'E saw me. Carm an' look fer yerself.

Iron They seem jaundiced Sweet'eart. I don't fink vey believe in yore guy wiv' blonde 'air.

Sweetheart Mister! Iss Five K 'ere. Five K fer cunts! We bin stuck 'ere all arternoon! An' 'ey ain't sent no one yet! We should 'ave 'ad Saulsby! By rights jus' now 'e should be climbin' out ver winders. But vere's just us an' iss gettin' a lit'l nasty. I mean, mister, we're teachin' ourselves dahn 'ere! You never know wot dangerous rubbish we might come up wiv'.

Skylight You got no need ter jream up assistance Sweet'eart. I know they fuckin' will.

Sweetheart 'E's turnin'. Turnin' away. 'E did look vis way. Looked me schraight in ve eye. But there's sunning goin' on ve ovver side a' the school. 'E's got ter go. 'E's walkin' away. 'Oi Mister. 'Don' go yet! Ve-ery slowly.

Pause.

You got ter come back Mister! You can't leave us like this!
You look a sympafetic sort a' geezer! Yore runnin' out on
us Mister! I mean vere's a lot you could tell us an' all in't
there? Mark Antony. Tell us abaht Mark Antony and
Cleopatra. We 'ad a geezer started ter tell us abaht Mark
Antony an Cleopatra on'y we 'it 'im wiv' an' 'ammer 'fore
'e 'ad a chance ter finish ver story! 'Oi Mister!

Pause.

Gone. Gone. Fuckin' gone. Clean away. Thass it. (*broken
up*) Fuckin' scab.

Skylight You always was seein' 'fings Sweetheart. 'E never
left us. 'E never was there. We ain't got no teacher wiv'
blonde 'air.

Sweetheart Door. I'll move away from the fuckin' door.
I'm finished. I'm bored tired sick wiv' doors an' waitin'.

Iron You'll stay by ver fuckin' door. You'll keep watch.
Thass yore job cunt. Ter watch. Ainch yoo proud a' that?
Ainch you got no pride. You stick at yore fuckin' job.

Sweetheart They jus' . . .

Iron Lissen. Donch you worry they're leavin' us 'igh an'
jry. Thass wot they done ter you the day you walked inter
this school wiv' one teacher ter four 'unjred pupils an' no
books an' nowhere ter fuckin' mess arahnd an' nuffink,
nuffink, zero, fuck all, *nuffink* 'ere. Donch you give me no
abandoned talk cunt. You was abandoned ver day you
was born 'ere ina block ten miles 'igh. Quit whinin'. Jus'
yoo get back ter that door an' let us know woch you see,
real and imaginary. We could do wiv' some fuckin'
entertainment.

Sweetheart Wot keeps you goin' Iron? I mean wot does?

Iron Biostrath cunt. As used by the stars. That an' the fact that I 'ate everyone. Now back ter ver door.

Skylight An' donch you worry. There'll be someone come along.

Iron Touchin' faith. Nuffing shatters our fat friend does it? Not even when 'is greasy 'aired tart –

Skylight Watch it.

Iron Wotch wot?

Skylight I *liked* 'er Iron. Or ainch you 'eard a' the word?

Iron Felt sorry for 'er didjer?

Skylight Maybe.

Iron You waste that stuff Skylight you know that? You can waste it. There's uvver things than feelin' sorry. Eh?

Skylight One day you'll understand Iron.

Iron Will I? Will I tell you all 'ow my ol' man's got a wooden leg an' lives in ver back of a Mini Minor off ve A23? Will I go on ver fuckin' stage? Will I be a bleed'n ballerina? Will I cry an' dance at the same time?

Sweetheart does a few joke ballet steps.

Sweetheart Da da da da-a.

Nipper Look at them bollocks.

Sweetheart Rudy this is. Rudy in the nudy.

Nipper moves to him.

Nipper Bollocks the size of apples.

Sweetheart An' abaht as useful. Da-da-da-a. 'Ver moon is full ternight!'

47

Nipper Not the on'y 'fing thass full friend.

Sweetheart 'Take your hands off me sailor lad.'

Nipper Is jus' ver sight a' yore –

Sweetheart becomes really annoyed.

Sweetheart Get *off*.

Nipper OK, OK.

Sweetheart Bleed'n perv.

Nipper So?

Iron 'E is too.

Nipper Class leper I am.

Skylight Yeh 'cos yore schoopid.

Racks 'Cos you fink blacks done it.

Iron Blacks never done it. Too bleed'n lazy. (*smile*) I'm
bored wiv' 'oo done it anyway. I don' 'fink we could any
longer describe it as the main point. I wanner know wot
we're gonna do back to 'em.

Racks To 'oo?

Nipper Blacks.

Iron Ah fuck off Nipper. Ter the cunts 'oo put us in this
dump. Why we bovver to argue 'oo. I tell you 'oo. Every
son of a cunt in the wide world 'cept us thass 'oo. Fuckin'
teachers an' fuckin' judges an' fuckin' mothers an' fuckin'
fathers an' fuckin' geezers on ver telly an' fuckin' doctors
an' fuckin' MPs an' fuckin' chraffic wardens, an –

Skylight Woss chraffic wardens ever done?

Iron They done plenty.

Skylight No one's fuckin' safe seems ter me.

48

Iron Maybe they ain't. Oh an' fuckin' popstars an' all. Pissin' off ter Epsom in white Rolls Royces an' comin' on they're workin' fuckin' class. Makes yer puke. Which brings me on ter bus conductors an' policemen oh Jesus Christ policemen –

Skylight Well if –

Iron Oh an' social workers an' all. Social workers are ver worst a' the fuckin' lot. I woun't leave a social worker alive if I 'ad my way. Problems. I'd give 'em problems. I'd sterilise 'em.

Racks Gordon Bennett 'e's off. I 'fought we was after knowledge 'ere.

Iron I'd 'ang up social workers by veir 'fumbs an' stick lighted candles between their toes. An' as fer their wives. Wot wouldn't I do ter social workers wives.

Skylight Anyway if –

Iron Oh an' while we're abaht it – lollipop men.

Skylight *Lollipop men?*

Iron Lollipop men.

Skylight They're nice are lollipop men. Lovely lit'l blokes. Wiv' white coats an' 'ats an' moustaches. I mean vey're blind mostly. So long as you don't cross the road anywhere near 'em I 'fink vere's a lot ter be said for lollipop men.

Iron Lollipop men will go. Inter ve acid barf wiv' bus conductors, policemen, pop-stars, estate-agents an' pet-shop owners an' second 'and cloves dealers an'–

Sweetheart Yore a one Iron aincher? You takin' ver piss or what?

Iron 'Oo's takin' ver piss? I mean it. I mean every word of it. Believe me I mean it. (*really angry*) You lot. You're fuckin' spineless.

Racks Not Skylight.

Iron Fuckin' jelly.

Skylight laughs.

See? Say anyfing you like to 'im 'e jus' laughs.

Sweetheart Somebody comin'.

Iron Yore like that geezer in ver Bible Skylight. Job. In ver Bible. They poured lava on 'is 'ead they 'ung 'im upside dahn in buckets a' shit, vey made 'im creosote san'wiches no good. Far as Job was concerned, vat was ace. That was great.

Sweetheart Somebody co-omin'.

Iron Woch you gotta learn Skylight is 'iss. You don' get up off your arse no teacher in ver world's goin' ter lift you up right? 'Iss you an' you only. No one else an' the on'y knowledge you –

Sweetheart Snatch. 'S Snatch.

Skylight Good lad.

Iron Reception committee.

Racks Uh?

Iron Line. Get in a fuckin' line.

Racks Woss up?

Iron Make a line lads. A line.

They respond to his drive again. And, when Snatch appears at the door, they're in a military style line. Iron goes to him and kisses him on both cheeks in the manner of one French general kissing a worthy soldier. The lads applaud. Skylight steps out and pins an imaginary medal on him. Finally the bewildered Snatch speaks.

Snatch 'Ullo.

Iron Welcome 'ome sailor.

Snatch 'Ullo.

Iron You are chruly welcome bruvver.

Racks Freedom a' the city.

Snatch Woss all 'iss 'en?

Racks Waste a' bleed'n time.

The group breaks up.

Iron Ain't they got no reformatories left then? Lettin' a vandal like you loose.

Sweetheart Welcome 'ome Snatch.

Snatch Woch you on abaht?

Iron 'S 'cos you parachuted inter France Snatch. An' lived fer firty-one days on a tin a baked beans.

Snatch I never.

Iron Modest an' all.

Skylight Yore a war 'ero Snatch.

Snatch War wot? (*grins, amiable*) I dunno.

Skylight Joke son. Never mind.

Iron Wot 'appened 'en Snatch?

Snatch Vey sent me back up 'ere.

Skylight Bloody 'ell.

Sweetheart I tolj yer. No need ter find no noo prisons.

Iron Warn yer did they?

Snatch Said not ter do it again.

Racks 'Ow many winders you break on yore way up Snatch?

Snatch None.

All Bollocks!

Snatch None. Honest. None.

Iron A reformed character. Ver system works. Ten years a' bashin' on ver bum an' social workers askin' fuckin' schoopid questions 'ave finally paid off. We are lookin' friends, at a reformed character. Rejoice.

Snatch I finished wiv' winders.

Iron 'Oooray 'ooray 'ooray. Blessed be ver Lord. Vis is why we still 'ave mornin' service friends.

Snatch Spray paint. 'Ass next. Cans a' fuckin' paint.

Iron Uh -uh.

Snatch Cans a fuckin' paint wiv' a brush. Thass it.

Skylight Snatch –

Snatch Yer –

Skylight Woch you done on yore way up 'ere?

Snatch I ain't done no winders.

Skylight Woch you done son?

Snatch Ahtside 4C vere's viss ladder. An' a fuckin' great tub a' white paint. An' a brush. An' nobody near 'em. So I goes up an' I picks up ver brush. Iss all 'eavy an' sticky an' nice. I picks it up an' bits a paint jrop off of it onter the parquet – two or 'free jrops – like a pattern. An' I looks

arahnd. No one arahnd. So I goes over ter the far wall an'
I jraw a fuckin' great S on it. Stand back. Looks great.
Fuckin' great. 'En I goes back again an' loads up me
brush. 'S all springy an' 'eavy when I done it. Like you
might imagine a gun or sunning. 'En I chrip back.
(*dreamy*) I wrote me name. I wrote SNATCH all across the
wall. In six foot letters all jrippin' dahn on ter the floor.
You can stan' back an' see it. SNATCH. Right up there.
Large as life. Don' talk ter me about no winders.

Iron We all got ter grow up eh?

Skylight Leave off of 'im.

Iron ' 'E's 'armless.'

Skylight 'E's 'armless.

Iron Donch you tell me that. I don' wanner know that.

Pause.

Maybe yore right. Growin' up eh? Join yer club Snatch.
You become a responsible vandal.

Snatch Fuckin' great.

Sweetheart 'Oo's next?

Snatch Woss 'iss?

Racks We're still givin' lessons. On'y now iss workin' out
why we're 'ere.

Snatch God put us 'ere.

Iron Oh fer cryin' out loud.

Skylight Leave *off* of 'im.

Sweetheart Tell you what. You put Snatch in next.

Racks Light relief.

53

Iron 'Fore the aggro starts eh Skylight?

Skylight There goin' ter be aggro Iron?

Iron I 'ad the impression you bin gearin' up to it this afternoon.

Snatch So wot do I teach yer?

Sweetheart Wocher like. We're all doin' it.

Snatch I don' know nuffink.

Sweetheart You mus' know sunnink.

Iron Carm on Snatch. Up there.

Snatch Well, I dunno. (*He stands in front of them.*) Wot do I do now?

Iron Talk.

Long pause.

Snatch Difficult innit?

Iron Wot?

Snatch Teachin'.

Iron Pushover.

Snatch I saw a bird in ver playground. A pigeon.

Iron Yes. And?

Snatch Well. I saw it.

Pause.

Vis is 'ard work Iron.

Iron Woch you care about Snatch? Woch you spend yore time doin'?

Snatch Doin'?

Pause.

Well. Till terday . . . . (*slow, amiable grin*) I done winders. Mainly.

Skylight OK. Winders. You giss a lesson on winders.

Snatch Can I? Can I really?

Racks I 'fought 'im an' winders was 'frough. Eh Snatch?

Snatch Well maybe . . .

Iron Snatch an' winders'll never be quite done will they Snatch? There'll always be a lit'l bit a' yore 'eart wiv' WINDERS written on it. Vandals may come an' vandals may go but there'll never be a love affair like you an' winders. Eh?

Snatch Can I really? Can I really talk about winders?

Sweetheart Pray silence fer friend Snatch 'oo's goin' ter talk abaht winders.

All 'OOR-AY!!

Snatch Right. Winders.

Pause.

I started on winders when I was in ve ovver school over by ver railway. Some cunt sez ter me in class "oo you bovverin' nigger?" jus' like that. No one ever called me that before. Nigger. I never 'eard it know what I mean? So I went 'ome I arxt ve ol' lady I sez 'Ma – woss it all abaht viss nigger?' She jus' laughed. But me Dad wuz furious an' 'en vey 'ad a row sayin' one 'fing arter anuvver an' 'fore they finished they was callin' each other nigger an' a lot of uvver 'fings beside. But it was funny. I din't like it. I din't like ver fuckin' word. Nigger. Jus' din't like it. An' I couldn't ferget it. So.

Pause.

I'm goin' ter school nex' day an' I pass vis shop dahn
Railton Road. 'Lectrics. Kettles an' at an' fires an' all. All
clean an' gleamin'. An' in ver middle 'ere's vis lit'l girl,
paper cut-out, wiv' gaps in 'er front teeth, grinnin' like on
ver telly. I stop. I look at vis girl. An' fer some reason I
don' like 'er. Iss like this. I'm stuck vere in Railton Road
an' everywhere roun' me is black people, black geezers in
a' doorways, black girls goin' to an' fro from ver launjrette
and black guys like my ol' man in cars – them square ones
– Austin Cambridge they are hundreds a' years old. An' in
'iss winder vere's vis paper cut-out girl an' she's white. I
mean so fuckin' white it makes yer sick.

Pause. They're listening to him as never before.

Well I 'fought ter meself 'Fuck you darlin'.' 'Cos it was like
she was sayin' one 'fing ter me you know? She was sayin'
'nigger' ter me like that kid in the class. There some ovver
people in a blow up photo be'ind 'er they was sayin'
'nigger' an' all. They was sayin' 'We got all ve electric
kettles an' fires an' anyfing we want so you fuck off black
boy.' So. I picks up vis stone an' chucks it. Warn't big
enough. I chucks anuvver. No good. Ven I gess me satchel
an' loads it up wiv' stones an' rubbish an' anyfing I can
find an' when the road's quiet I swing it round an' round
an' then let go – like *that*. Oh. You shoulda seen that glass.
Shoulda *seen* it. (*dreamy*) Bes' time fer winders is 'free in
ver mornin' when no one's abaht.

Iron Go *on*.

Snatch Uh?

Iron Go *on*.

Snatch Wot?

Iron We like it. We *like* it.

56

Snatch Yeh?

Pause.

Skylight We do Snatch. But not the way 'e means it.

Snatch Yeah. Ver schreet's quiet an' out I goes. Since my ol' man flung me out I'm in ve 'ostel right? But I crack out of it no problem. Iss OK vere but . . . anyway. Iss all quiet an' 'ere's jus' me wiv' arf a brick wrapped in clof' case ver Blues see me. Iss best you stand back ten yards and chuck. It can be dang'rous 's 'cos when it shatters you gotta be careful see? Well.

Pause.

First of all I done Woolies in ve 'Igh Schreet. 'En I done John Lewis that was. 'En I done a chip-shop back a' the main station. 'En I done a couple a' small ones up Brixon 'Ill. Now I go anywhere. I done Tescos. I done Sainsbury's. I done W. H. Smif's. I done ver Co-op. I done Rumbelow's 'Lectric shop. I done 'free John Wests, two Whitbread's Offs, a pub up Streatham, ver Chransport Museum, Clapham Barves, a parked bus, John Menzies, 'free Odeons, a Gaumont an' a corner shop by ver station wot sells wine.

Pause.

'Vis geezer I met wiv' was tellin' me abouta place called 'Arrods. 'Pparently at 'Arrods vey 'ave abaht sixteen fuckin' great winders wiv' all sorts in 'em an' 'fings that light up – plate glass every fuckin' one. So thass on my list. Fuckin' 'Arrods.

Long pause.

I done now.

Skylight You done all right Snatch.

57

Snatch Finished?

Iron Yer. You finished.

Skylight You done all right Snatch.

Iron You done brilliant Snatch. Skylight says so.

Snatch Yeh?

Iron You ever 'eard a' Oxford University Snatch?

Snatch No.

Iron No. I 'fought not. Well Snatch – I reckon on the basis a' that lesson you could 'ave a very promising career there. An' as friend Skylight said – you done well. You spoke, Snatch, wiv' eloquence, an' I feel, *Pofessor* Snatch that if we could teach you to read we –

Skylight Leave off of 'im.

Iron Why? Why leave off of 'im? Woss so great about bein' a schoopid black cunt 'oo breaks winders eh? Wot makes you carry on like someone's muvver eh? You pat people on the back fer bein' 'uman you do Skylight.

Skylight So?

Iron So. Woss so fuckin' great abaht bein' 'uman?

Snatch 'Ere. I'm 'uman. Jus'. Thass wot my ol' man says.

Iron See?

Skylight I see nuffink. You let me get on wiv' wot I wanner do. You leave off a' me with this needlin' you bin up to all afternoon. Donch you make your problems mine.

Iron Well my problems are your problems cunt. On account we live free schreets away from each ovver you big dumb wanker. Remember?

A new note of tension. Skylight sounds as if he's rising to

58

the bait. Sweetheart tries to deflate things with a joke.

Sweetheart 'Ere. I'll do my Angela Rippon.

Iron No you fuckin' won't.

Sweetheart I'll do my Reginald Bosanquet.

Iron You won't do nuffink a' the kind. You'll do your deaf, dumb and blind act an' you'll keep an eye on that door. We're gonna get some knowledge now from Professor Skylight woss gonna make it all worf' while. Words a' wisdom will make wings sprout in the small of our bleed'n backs.

Skylight Stony ground Iron.

Iron Yeah I'm stony ground cunt. Now you plant me.

Skylight I gave up on you Iron –

Iron Well don't cunt. Fuckin' –

Skylight You ain' worf' no lesson Iron you ain' worf' –

Iron I 'fought you was all fer everyone bein' great Skylight. I was under the impression that you reckoned everyone was in wiv' arf a chance if on'y they lissned ter you an' was nice to ol' ladies an' cats an' dogs an' people in wheelchairs.

Skylight Iron you – (*decides to go ahead*) Ah shit. Why not?

Iron 'E's gonna do it everybody. Professor Skylight from ver University a' Oxford is goin' ter tell us 'ow everyfing is goin' ter be OK. 'E's gonna tell us 'ow No one Done It an' Nuffink Needs ter be Done. 'E's gonna make us cry boys an' girls.

Skylight Finished?

Iron Fer the moment.

Skylight Right. Shall we begin?

Iron Be – egin!

Skylight An' I'll 'ave order in my class you lit'l twerp. Geddit!! Order. Or you'll be done over good an' proper. OK? Twerp?

Iron stays quite still.

See? I can shout. Any cunt can shout.

Iron Any cunt can apologize an' all.

Skylight I am not apologizing you lit'l prick! Take that! OK? Twerp? OK?

He hits Iron across the face. Iron doesn't react. Iron's waiting for something more than this. But he won't take too much.

Iron Stea-ady.

Skylight I am steady! I am fuckin' steady!

Iron Ea-asy boy. You –

Skylight I am so sorry Iron I do apologize I mus' say I am so sorry Iron really! (*Looks as if he's going to hit him again. Doesn't. Pats him on the cheek.*) Sorry.

Iron Teach cunt. Teach.

Skylight Professor Skylight a' Oxford University. Begins.

Sweetheart I wanner go.

Skylight You stay put.

Sweetheart I wanner go.

Pause. He is very frightened.

I jus' wanner . . .

Racks Knowledge. Very scary is knowledge. ✓

Iron You 'eard Teacher. Stay put.

Sweetheart sits.

Skylight Prepare ter learn sunnink useful.

All Yes Teacher!

Iron If we like it.

Skylight You give it a chry Iron. Give it a chry. Nah. (*Pulls out a desk.*) In 'ere I 'ave . . . ternight's dinner.

Racks Fuckin' cookery lesson.

Iron Domestic science Skylight. You got an apron wiv' yer?

Skylight From my desk I take . . . ver raw materials. (*He takes out a plastic bag containing a sliced loaf, a bottle of milk, some currants and a half a pound of butter.*) Anyone got a box?

Racks 'Ere yer are.

Skylight Now lads. We are goin' ter learn 'ow ter make a Great British Dish. Otherwise known as Bread an' Butter Pudd'n.

All Shame! Ru-bbish!

Skylight Sssh.

Pause.

Nah. Ver great 'fing abaht Bread an' Butter Puddin' is 'iss. Vere ain't no meat in it. I 'ear you ask "Ow come?" an' I answer you – 'because you can't afford meat'. So woss ver point of a meal wiv' meat? Ridiculous the very idea. Two quid fer a piece a' lamb wot won't fill yer up eh? Woss ver use?

Iron Let 'em eat cake eh Skylight?

Skylight Now that I didn't say. I said you 'appen, you jus' 'appen ter be eatin' bread an' butter puddin' on account you gotter take out a fuckin' mortgage you wanner eat meat. Right? An' in ver absence a' the fuckin' Meat Mortgage Company – mos' of us ain' eatin' it. But, Iron, we are eatin' Bread an' Butter Puddin'. An' we might as well make the bleedin' best of it.

Pause.

Because. Bread an' Butter Puddin' can be beautiful. It can be like ver Swiss Alps on a spring mornin' an Rome in autumn can Bread an' Butter Puddin'. O ve ovver 'and it can be like a goat's bum. *If* you don't make it right. So instead a' fuckin' money moanin' let us get on wiv' the business a' seein' *'Ow It Is Done.*

Nipper 'Ey Skylight? You ver fam'ly chef then?

Skylight As it 'appens I am. Now. (*Holds up packet of butter.*) First ingredient. Butter.

Iron Geddaway.

Skylight Now. Don' go mad wiv' ver butter on account they ain't givin' it away.

Iron Marvellous. Marvellous. Calls it sunning an' butter puddin' firs' 'fing you do is 'old back on one a' the main numbers. Woch you use fer bread then Skylight on account bread's so dear? Rubber bands? I mean if you put someone in a tin and call it Buckingham Palace does that 'elp keep yer rain out? I mean fer Chrissake Professor you sound you're set on lies not knowledge on a –

Skylight 'Oo's givin' 'iss lesson cunt? Me or you?

Iron You are. Badly.

Skylight You shut your face an' you'll learn sunning! Becos' wevver I make it wiv' bindweed an' cyanide or crisp packets an' 'orses bollocks 'iss is Bread n' Butter Puddin'. Just the same way my ol' man's four second 'and books on a done over cardboard box as far as 'e's fuckin' concerned, is 'is fuckin' library.

Iron Your ol' man mus' be a slow reader Professor.

Skylight 'E is cunt. On account of 'e reads wiv' 'is fuckin' fingers. On account 'e's fuckin' blind.

Iron Oh save me. Save me. Oh Gawd, I don' believe it. 'Iss is too much. I will break down. 'Is ol' man's blind. Oh Jesus. A white stick an' all. Oh fuck me. You're 'avin' us on. Oh we must be goin' barmy. This is so movin'. Oh Gordon Bennett.

Skylight You 'frough cunt?

Iron Oh yeh. I'm 'frough. I'm done. I'm sorry Professor. I knoo was a saint in jrag. Oh 'elp us all. Tell me though. One thing. 'Fore you carry on tellin' us 'ow ter make Wood an' Treacle puddin' or whatever you call it tell me – is your ol' lady by any chance wivout peepers an' all.

Skylight As a matter of fact cunt – she is.

This is the funniest thing Iron's ever heard.

Iron Oh thass good. 'Iss good. No wonder you never let me rounj yore 'ouse. Oh save us, 'ass fuckin' great. Oh no. No more. Skylight's Mum and Dad bumpin' inter ver furniture an' Skylight in the corner makin' Bread an' Butter Puddin'. 'Ass too much. Iss *fantastic*. Iss incredible. Oh. Oh stop it. Oh no. More. Please. *Issterical.* (*looks round at the class*) I mean wot a bleed'n bunch a' derelicts we turned aht ter be eh? Eh? I mean ain' we jus' a social worker's fuckin' jream come chroo. Oh Jesus. Jesus H.

63

Christ. (*still laughing*) You 'ave ter fuckin' laugh. You 'ave ter fall abaht really. Doncher? Eh?

Skylight Like I said cunt I intend to teach a lesson. If you intend ter fuckin' learn then lissen.

Racks 'Ey. I don' 'fink they *do* like each uvver. You know?

Sweetheart Look can't we –

Iron Ah. When you 'ate each uvver ver way the Professor an' I do iss like love innit Professor? Innit?

Sweetheart Look. No one minds a row but –

Skylight Look. I'm teachin'. I'm gettin' on wiv it. Nah. (*back to his ingredients*) Right. Firs' of all you take yer bakin' tin. Like so. (*takes an empty box off the sill*) An you scrub it rahnd wiv' butter. Like so. Plen'y of it but not too much. An' 'en you take a bit a' bread an' butter, buttering the bread on bof' sides.

Iron Watch the money there Skylight!

Skylight Shuch yer face an' watch. (*He's buttering the bread, just one piece*) 'En we place ver bit a bread at ver bottom of ver pan like so. An' we do the same wiv' anuvver bit a bread until ve 'ole a' the bakin' tin is covered.

Racks Thass a big pan you got there Skylight.

Skylight We'll take it as read son, ovverwise I ain' gonna eat ternight am I? So. 'Ere you are, wiv a layer a' bread. Then – ver raisins. You shake aht the raisins on top a' the bread like so. An' you do the same all the way up.

Iron 'Ey Professor – yer bein' a bit tight wiv' ver raisins. You worried abaht Mum an' Dad's dinner? Carm on. Vey won' notice. Wocher don' see yer don't miss. Carm on son. Less give yer a 'and. (*Starts to shake his arm. Too many raisins come out.*) Less 'ave yer. Less –

64

Skylight Fuck off! (*Pushes him back. Hard.*) Leave off eh?

Iron Well you tell me! Woss so fuckin' important abaht a few fuckin' raisins! I mean is it right you should be be 'ere worryin' abaht a few fuckin' raisins when 'ere's cunts in Chelsea 'frowin' away fuckin' steak! Is it? I mean is that justice?

Skylight I ain't talkin' abaht justice! I'm talkin' abaht my fuckin' dinner! OK?

Pause.

An' now boys an' girls. If you will allow me. I will add the sugar. Like so. On ter the top like so. An' 'en all the way up ter the top see? Nah. When you got enough pieces you pour yer milk over as it might be like that an' leave it all ter soak. Nice long time. Oh you gotter add egg ter ver milk.

Racks Why?

Skylight Bind it.

Nipper Blimey.

Skylight Bake in a moderate oven fer about as long as it takes ter jrink two pints. Then eat – makin' sure the juice dribbles dahn yer chin. A delicious dish friends. Ideal for intimate supper parties or for an' evenin' a' TV viewin'. If you are really plannin' on goin' wild go an' buy some chips an' all.

Iron My ol' Du-utch!

Skylight Nex' week. Mince an' Gravy. 'Ow ter serve it in a way that will be a credit to your 'ome. Send now for a full colour leaflet of uvver specialities of the 'ouse – includin' Big Tin a' Beans, Small Tin a' Beans, One Sausage, Two Sausages, 'Free Sausages an' do not forget Eggs So Many Ways It Makes Yer Puke. I thankyeeow.

Ragged applause.

Iron Wot der they do then Skylight? Sit there wiv' their
mouves open while you jrop it in? I mean you told me
your ol' man was a –

Skylight Never mind wot I fuckin' tolj yer. An you shut up
now. O.K?

Iron I will by no means shut up Professor Skylight. You
see I ain't satisfied wiv' ver bit a' knowledge you gave us. I
mean I wanner know a lot more'n 'ow ter stick a bit a'
Wonderloaf in a fuckin' pan. I wanner know *why* you're
stickin' Wonderloaf in a fuckin' pan. I wanner know
wevver you 'fink iss right you should be doin' all 'at
cookin' son. I wanner know all about that simple joy you
feel at the sight a' your sightless parents forkin' yore
delicious food inter their ears an' everywhere but in their
fuckin' mouves I wanner know why you never told me
nuffink abaht yore fuckin' parents I wanner know –

Skylight I never tolj you nuffink Iron. Like none of us ever
told each ovver nuffink. Buch you special. Even when we
was 'alfway ter mates I never tolj you nuffink. You know
why?

Pause.

'Cos I can't trust you. I can't trust you ter take nuffing the
way iss meant. 'Cos you're twisted. Twisted. I know you
Iron. You say we're tellin' sob stories. But iss you makes
every fuckin' 'fing into a sob story. You miss so much out
doncher? You jus' don' understand an' you never 'ave.

Iron Fuck off.

Skylight Oh you get enough ter get riled. But thass it.
Stops there dunnit? You know wot I reckon? I reckon they
left sunnin' out a' you when they puch yer on ver market.

66

Iron Fuck off.

Skylight You know 'oo you're soundin' like? Friend Nipper.

Iron Nipper?

Skylight Yeh.

Iron Fuck off.

Skylight This lesson could go on fer years Iron but I'd never get it right. I mean you'd shuch yore fuckin' ears to it wouncher? I could tell you abaht jraught lager an' brahn ale an' why one beats ve ovver 'cos a' the way they taste an' 'ow you feel good when you jrink 'em but you don' wanner know do yer? 'Cos all you feel is riled. Thass all yore fuckin' inchrested in innit? An' 'ow you gonner pick up all this bleed'n knowledge when you're riled eh? 'Ow you gonner concentrate? You tell me that.

Iron *Lissen –*

Skylight Now I'll tell you about my ol' man an' my ol' lady an' it ain't no sob story so donch yoo come the fuckin' sneers on it OK?

Sweetheart Ah patch it up lads eh?

Skylight You know why I never arst yer back? You know why I never mentioned 'em. 'Cos there ain't so much ter mention. I mean. They was blind when they met right?

Iron My o-old Du-utch!

Skylight Thass all over. But my ol' man an' my ol' lady –

Iron 'An' it don't seem a day too-oo much!'

Skylight *Like* each ovver. 'Member that word Iron? Like. Wot I do ter bread an' butter puddin'. Wot Racks does ter gardenin'. Like. Chry an' remember that word. An' even if

67

my ol' man an' my ol' lady's like a couple a' prunes kissin'.
Well. Isn't that better than two prunes lyin' side by side an'
starin' at the ceilin'. Iss better 'an yore ol' lady done up
like a dog's dinner 'cos the poor ol' git's lookin' fer it an'
yore ol' lady fer Chrissake likes a glass she 'as a good time
when she sets 'er mind to it. An' even 'ere where the
schreets are paved wiv' shit on account they ran outta gold
an' sometimes they don' send you no teachers fer days an'
days an' days well iss *livin'* innit? Iss better'n bein' dead fer
a start.

Iron 'Oo knows? I never chried bein' dead. Bein' dead
might be great. It might be parties every night.

Skylight I mean you waste yourself Iron. You know that?
Waste yourself. You do though. 'Cos when it comes down
to it all you do is rabbit rabbit rabbit. You're a mess. You
don' know 'oo yore friends are do yer?

Iron My frien's are the cunts 'oo 'ate my enemies.

Skylight Gawd.

Iron Learn this Professor. The world is divided, more or
less equally, between wankers an' cunts. Wankers are a bit
better'n cunts but at any moment they can slip back. They
ain't guaranteed. OK? Nah shut up an' teach us sunning
useful.

Skylight I'm teachin' you sunning useful. But you ain't
learnin' are yer? You ain't willin' ter learn. You ain't
inchrested in livin' let alone learnin'. Are yer?

Iron Well. You're goin' ter 'ave ter teach a lit'l bit 'arder
aincher?

Skylight Oh I'm patient. I'll be as patient as you like. But
sooner or later yore gonna 'ave ter melt yore 'ead a lit'l bit.
You're gonna 'ave ter bend that stiff fuckin' neck a' yours.
Aincher?

Sweetheart I'm definitely off.

Skylight Sta-ay. (*grabbing him*) Stay boy. Stay.

Racks Surprise surprise.

Nipper Nah this is wot we bin waitin' for innit?

Skylight Well. Friend Iron said it din't 'e? Or if he din't 'e should a done. Knowledge ends in a punch up don' it? The on'y way ter teach a cunt 'oo won't learn is ter tie 'im ter the floor an' 'frow darts at 'im. Thass friend Iron's message innit? An' I'm willin' ter teach.

Iron Iss bin comin' ter you a long time Skylight.

Skylight Maybe so.

Iron You can still back off you want to.

Skylight I can't wait Iron. Ter teach you the joys a' life.

Iron Tell me that when I've broke yore legs.

Skylight I'll tell you that you pull my innards out an' 'ang 'em up ter dry. I tell you that any hour a' the day. You can't stop me Iron. People will go on livin' an' likin' it. Ain' it all a bleed'n shame.

Iron Coat off cunt.

Skylight Circle.

Racks Lissen –

Skylight Chicken on my account?

Racks Skylight you ain't got –

Skylight Not worried abaht me are yer Racks?

Racks You ain't – (*shakes head*) Jesus.

Iron Circle lads. Push back ver fuckin' desks.

Snatch 'Ere. A punch-up.

Iron To end all punch-ups.

Skylight Circle.

Iron Less 'ave you.

They form a group around Iron. Then the fight starts. It should be very realistic. Slow. Boxing jabs. A couple of attempts at a wrestling grip. Suddenly Iron goes in close and they're both on the floor. The group closes in. We can't see them.

Racks Break 'em.

They're pulled apart and set up again like a couple of boxers. Skylight's nose is bleeding.

Iron Life still great cunt? Life still lovely is it?

Skylight Fuckin' beautiful Iron. Like Ancient fuckin' Persia.

Iron Less 'ave you.

The fight starts again. They're both on the floor.

Racks Pull 'im off!

Snatch Leave 'em.

Racks 'E'll kill 'im!

Snatch Stand away.

Racks Carm *on*.

Racks and Sweetheart pull up Iron. The two are stood up again but this time Skylight takes his time. He is cut really badly. Blood coming from above his eye.

Leave off now eh?

Sweetheart Yeh. Leave it.

Skylight Fuck off cunt.

Iron There Skylight. You learnin' yire lesson?

Skylight I'm teachin' Iron. Remember?

Iron Cunt.

He goes for him really wild. Gets him on the ground and starts to bang his head against it. The group closes in. Snatch too.

Racks Fer Gawd's sake.

This time Skylight does not get up. The group clears and we see Skylight centre stage. Badly beaten up.

Iron OK then. Now say it. Say you learn your lesson. Say you learned 'ow 'fings pan out dahn 'ere. Say you know they won't send no one. Never. Say it.

Skylight Get fucked.

Iron Lissen –

Racks Leave off of 'im Iron.

But Skylight is getting up. With great difficulty.

Skylight Now. If I may go on with the lesson.

Iron goes to him.

Iron Donch yoo know when yore beat cunt? Donch yoo know when wot you sez sounds fuckin' schoopid? Donch yoo know when jribblin' on abaht the beauty a' nacher sounds plains daft? Donch yoo?

Skylight Nope.

Iron Donch you know when you've learned your fuckin' lesson you schoopid git?

Skylight Like I said Iron. I'm still teachin'.

71

Iron goes for him. As he does so the **Master** *comes in from the back. The two break and face the front.*

Master What's going on here?

Snatch Nothing sir please sir.

Nipper Please sir a fight sir.

Master You. Skellet is it?

Iron Me sir?

Master I don't know. Here boy.

Skylight Woof woof.

Master Bloody insolent little – (*Goes for him. Sees his face.*) Jesus Christ.

Skylight You rang sir.

Master Savages. You little savages.

Skylight Didjer want sunning sir?

Master Come with me.

Skylight Where to sir?

Master For God's sake. Who started this?

Skylight No one sir.

Master Who –

Skylight No one sir.

Master I give up on kids like you. I give up. It really is like going down into the bear pit. Did you know that?

Skylight No sir.

Master We don't teach you do we? We throw you bits of information – like bones and you quarrel over them? Did you know that?

72

Skylight No sir.

Master Do you just grunt to each other when you're alone. Like animals. Eh? I give up on you I really do.

Skylight Yes sir.

Master I give up teaching you do you know that?

Skylight I know that sir. You give up teaching us.

Master Are you being insolent Skellet?

Skylight No sir.

Master I just . . . Jesus. You better come.

Skylight No sir. Thank you sir.

Master Come *on* –

Iron Hands off 'im cunt.

Master I beg your pardon?

Iron You 'eard wot I said – 'ands off of 'im.

Master What is your name?

Iron Iron's my name cunt.

Master Listen. For the moment I'm going to ignore your foul language and ask you once again, for your proper name.

Iron Iron, cunt. An' donch yoo ferget it.

Master *Right* –

Iron Right what?

Master I think you need a –

Iron Don' touch me cunt. Or you'll get done. 'Ere an' now. An' later too when you walk outta school. OK? We 'eard you. You give up on us. Well we give up on you cunt

73

an' we mean it. You lay a finger on me an' I'll damage you proper.

Master *I* remember you.

Iron Do you cunt?

Master Herron. That's your name. Yes.

Pause.

Do you know Herron that I find people like you the most depressing of the lot. Because you're really very bright aren't you. But you throw it all away. You don't *want* to know do you? You just don't want to know.

Iron Know what cunt?

Master Dumb insolence or downright insolence I tell you I give up.

Snatch Please sir I'm sorry sir.

Master Uh?

Snatch Please sir I'm sorry sir.

Master What?

Snatch 'Bout wot I done on ver wall sir.

Master *What* exactly did you do on the wall Cameron?

Snatch My name sir. Snatch sir. I done my name.

Master Well Cameron, I don't know whether this means anything to you but I don't care about the wall. I didn't come here to complain about the wall or about whatever you may have done to it. I didn't actually intend to come here at all Cameron. I *happened* to be passing. Because if you want to know wild horses wouldn't drag me anywhere near this particular hell hole in the normal course of events. And Cameron, after what you little savages have done to the doors, windows and walls of this school I don't think one more name or one more foul word is going to make any difference whatsoever. You see, Cameron – we've given up caring about what the place looks like. We've given up caring Cameron.

Pause.

I think if we put you lot in the Garden of Eden – in ten minutes you'd have it looking like a slum. If we put you in the middle of Buckingham Palace you'd lay it waste just as speedily and thoroughly as you do this poor benighted, last post of education.

Iron Yeh. We could cunt. An' yoo know why?

Master No Herron. You tell me why.

Iron 'Cos ve on'y 'fing we don' lay waste to is ours. An' nuffink's ours. You ain't given us nuffink an' wot you give us you take away at your convenience. An' as long as you treat us that way we'll lay waste cunt. Books, teachers, winders, doors, walls, floors, we'll lay it all ter waste. 'Till we get sunning thass ours. OK cunt?

Master You're not fit for ownership Herron. You're not fit to be trusted with each other. Are you coming Skellet?

Skylight No I ain't.

Master Come on.

Skylight Don't touch me sir. Or like 'e said. You'll get done.

Master Honour among thieves eh? Eh?

Skylight On'y fuckin' place there is any honour. Sir.

Master There. Well I wouldn't expect anyone else. I don't think we've got anyone to send down to you. I think, frankly, that you'd be better off in the streets don't you?

Isn't that what the police are for? Because this, in case you hadn't noticed, is a place of learning, a place you come to to acquire knowledge. And it is only the knowledge that you brought in with you that you will take away. The knowledge of how to bully, swear and break. Yes?

Pause.

I give up on you. We give up on you. It's pathetic. Did you know that? It's not funny or brave or clever or angry or anything. It's pathetic. (*at door*) I should clear off if I were you. Just leave. *Leave.*

He goes. When he's gone Iron whips round to the front of the class.

Iron Ye-eahh!!

But no one is interested in war dances. They don't approve of what he did to Skylight.

Iron's lesson now lads. Last lesson. One more river. Iron'll *teach* yer sunning. Won' 'e?

No response.

Self defence. Thass ol' Iron's lesson. Now. Firs' position. Feet flat on ver floor arms out 'ere an' broken bottle a' Tizer 'ere. Come on lads, 'iss is it – ver lesson you bin waitin' for. Ol' Iron – ver revealed word a' God. Carm on. Fightin'.

But he's lost them. Nipper and Sweetheart still with him.

Ver are two kin's a fight. Those yer win an' those yer lose. Now you take Jeff Darby up Carradon Gardens – big bloke, great boxin' style. Up against a punch-bag 'e looks great. Up against a real live 'uman – fuckin' useless. 'Fing abaht a fight – *any* fight – is ter move first. Nuffink ter do wiv' 'ow big they are or 'ow big you are. Move first. Go fer the soft bits. Now take me. I'm 'ere an' Nipper's there –

76

well I don' 'fink 'if I go fer 'is 'froat 'e might go fer mine an' 'at 'urts.' I go. Schraight fer 'is fuckin' 'froat. An' 'e's on ver fuckin' floor 'fore 'e knows I got a fuckin' 'froat. Nah come on lads – less 'ave someone from the audience.

No takers.

Come on. 'Iss is it. Iron's lesson. Valuable stuff. Top a' the bleed'n bill. Come *on*. Gawd; what a bunch. Donch yoo wanner know? Donch yoo wanner know 'ow ter punch back? Eh? You owe a few punches doncher? I mean you're fuckin' owed 'arf an hour's worth a' jumpin' up an' dahn on people's stomachs. Carm on you spineless cunts show some fuckin' inchrest in fuckin' self defence. (*Takes up position.*) Nah. Someone comes up ter yer right? Wiv' a left. 'Ere 'e is. 'Ere's 'is left. An' you block it right? You block it. An' 'en your lef' foot goes in 'ere right? 'Tween 'is. An' 'en like so wiv' ve elbow – like *so*. 'Ass used that is. Used in the American Army. I read it. Fuckin' used. 'Swell known. OK. 'E's on ver floor. Well *lissen* you cunts. Pay some bleed'n attention you load a' women. Lend me yore fuckin' ears. This is knowledge this is. This gonna be some fuckin' use out vere innit? Carm *on*.

Even Nipper and Sweetheart have turned away. Racks is looking after Skylight.

Nah. 'E's dahn. An' you are gonna stan' back? Do you stand back like Gentlemen Jims? 'Oh I am sorry I hit you. Do get up.' Or do you go in there? Well you fuckin' go in there. You get the boot in. No messin'. An' you get the boot in *hard* OK? I'm goin' 'ome two weeks ago wiv' a lit'l geezer from over ver road an' two guys come out an' jump 'im. Nut 'im. Like 'at. Woss 'e do? I'll tell you wot 'e does. 'E fuckin' apologizes. 'I'm sorry,' 'e says. 'I'm so sorry.' An' thass us innit? We apologize. Fer livin' 'ere. Even ter cunts like wot jus' walked 'frough 'ere.

77

Racks I din't notice no one apologizin' Iron.

Iron Women. You lot. Bunch a' women. There 'e is on ver floor. Nah. Someone else comes up be'ind yer. You can 'ear 'im see? Like this. You don' turn. You wait. You can feel 'im. Prickles on ver back a' the neck sez 'e's there right be'inj yer. So you wait. An' wait. An' 'en *BANG* . . . you got 'is 'and. 'E's schruggling' buch yoo boot back. An'. Boot back an' 'e's dahn. An' 'en you go back. Back over 'im. Feet first right?

Sweetheart Anuvver one be'inj yer Iron.

Iron *There*. Right. Over. Schraight between ve eyes. Real smash. Blood on 'is fuckin' face. Done 'im. 'S two a' 'em laid out.

Racks Watch it Iron. 'Ere's anuvver one.

Iron An' *there* 'e goes. Back you cunts. Two more. Two fuckin' more keepin' yer feet fair an' square nicely solid they can't move me off my fuckin' feet no way I tell you that friends I keep four square an' I'm waitin' . . .

Racks Lookout!

Iron Gocha!

Nipper An' anuvver one!

Snatch An' anuvver!

Iron Fuck off willyer! (*backing; alone centre stage*) All a' yer! Fuck off you spineless cunts! One step near me an' I'll damage yer OK? Now mark this well! Mark this fuckin' well! Be very careful 'cos I'll take yer! I'll take yer you don' watch it! OK? (*punching the air*) There. There. An *there*.

Skylight 'Oo's there Iron?

Iron You know 'oo's fuckin' there son. You know it.

There. An' a rap wiv' a left an' *schraight* out – cover
yerself – keep movin'. You fuckin' know it doncher?
Fuckin' teachers an' lawyers an' social workers an' schreets
an' 'ouses an' judges an' teachers you name it they're there.
Everyone's fuckin' there cunt. Woah – you sod. Back off.
An' tap 'im wiv' ver left. Keep dancin'. Dancin'. (*He's
boxing his own shadow.*) Yeh. Movin' 'em back 'en I?
Move ver cunts back. Ol' Iron. Self-defence. Now 'ere's a
fuckin' lesson for yer you cunts a lesson you shoulda
learned a long way back so you be oh so very careful
when you talk ter me. *There.* Rap.

Skylight Take 'em all on Iron eh?

Iron I'll keep it up cunt. I'm ve on'y one 'ere in 'iss 'ol
black fuckin' dump 'oo will. On'y one in 'iss unsuitable bit
a' bleed'n desert 'oo will 'ave a punch back. On'y one 'oo
speaks up fer 'issself eh? On'y one 'oo 'as any guts. So keep
off. Keep off. Guard down. See? I can play it easy now.
Relax. I can relax. There they are. I got 'em waitin'. Iron's
game. One step ahead. Waitin'. Judge it. Fuckin' goons.
You wait there cunts. (*a scream*) Well come on 'en! Less
'ave yer! Don' jus' stand there! Fuckin' finish me if yore
gonna finish me! I'll take you on no problem! Not ter
worry donch you worry 'bout me! (*suddenly desperate*)
Ple-e-ease!!

Skylight turns to him.

Skylight Joo remember them records Iron? Them records?
You was always off buyin' records werencher – in ver days
when you an' me was talkin' to each ovver. An' each
fuckin' time it was the same thing. You'd get ver sod back
an' play it 'frough. Great. It sounded great. So off you'd
go an' play it again an' it'd be great. But twice wasn't it
was it? You'd play it again an' that time I 'member you'd
always say 'Skylight' you'd say – 'that was great. Great.
But I can't stand it. Quite.' An' after that you'd 'ave ter

play it again and again and again until you couldn't stand ver fuckin' sight of it. Then you was finished wiv' it werencher? You loathed it. Someone else could 'ave it eh? If I din't know better I'd a' said that fer you lissenin' ter fuckin' music was like an operation wivout benefit a' anaesthetic. It was like you was shut out of it an' no matter 'ow 'arj you pushed you was never gonna get inside.

Iron I tell you no one gets under me! No one gets past my fuckin' guard you load a fuckin' *women*!!

Iron goes, quite literally, berserk. Smashing desks, ripping up books, smashing everything he can see, heading for his classmates, screaming and sobbing and swearing. When he's finished there is more violence out of him than at any other time in the play and he sounds almost vulnerable. He turns to Skylight.

Why joo do it Skylight? Why joo let me 'it you like that? I din't fuckin' mean it. Honest. I never fuckin' mean it. I jus' go on. On an' on an' on an' on an' on an' on. An' I don' add up do I? I don' make sense.

Pause. They're listening to him now.

Nah. Donch you run away wiv' ve idea ol' Iron's gone soft. Nah. Me? I can stil lick 'oo I like carn I? I'm no one's fool. I do as I like. Still fuckin' boss 'ere anyrate. Still fuckin' boss. I ain't apologizing. You lissen ter me 'cos I tell wot 'appens eh? 'Ow it is an' you better fuckin' face it. (*feeling their hostility again*) Nobody messes me abaht! Anytime I can do you Skylight! Anytime I want I'll lay you out son onver fuckin' floor ter get one message 'frough yore 'ead someone lumbered us wiv' bein' 'ere an' we ain't standin' for it we're gonna break out of 'ere no question! We're gonna go over ver river an' we're gonna smash an' break an' burn an' kill ev'ry rich cunt we find we're gonna be so fuckin' dangerous vey won' know wot 'it 'em. Y'ou stick wiv' me! You 'ang arahnd or I'll teach yer ver same lesson over an' over again until vere's blood comin' ouch yore ears until you know wot it fuckin' feels like ter be ground down by a pack a' sods! Well look at me you spineless cunts! Look at me! Or are you afraid I'll 'ich yer if you look at me! I got a message fer you I got some fuckin knowledge fer you you bastard load a' half-wit girls! (*He falters. And, once again, that note of weakness, creeping into his voice. A desperate longing to be liked underneath it all.*) Lissen. I ain' got no fuckin' knowledge. I jus' ask don' I? Ask and ask and ask an' punch an' I don' get no fuckin' nearer do I? Nuffink adds up nuffink makes sense not one thing means anyfing I jus' punch an' punch an' punch an' wot is there? Nuffink. Jus' fuck all. No answers from no one. Jus' useless fuckin' Iron wiv' a load a' useless fuckin' questions. Ah knowledge. No one got knowledge. Ain't no fuckin' knowledge to be 'ad nowhere in ver wide fuckin' world.

Skylight Iron you lissen ter me. Listen close. 'Cos someone'll come. Someone will walk 'frough vat door. Fer us. 'Course vey will. I ain't sayin' vere ain' no bad apples. Bad apples in every bunch. But in ver main . . . in ver main . . . people come out. They do right by yer given 'arf a chance. They don' sit back and lech yer rot. 'Cos in the main they fuckin' care. 'Course vere's bad apples. But in ver main they care. Thass wott I'm sayin'. An' sure as I'm standin' 'ere talkin' ter you, sure as night follers day in five minutes or ten minutes or fifteen minutes or any rate pretty fuckin' soon we're gonna get visited. An' 'oo's ter know. Nex' time they might be the bes' we' ad yet. They might be top-class. They might be God's gift never know. We might never argue when vere 'ere. We might jus' know. An' 'oo's ter know – they might come on wiv' so much fuckin' knowledge we won't be able ter move fer knowledge. We'll 'ave arrived Iron. All you need in this world is patience. Swear it to you. You can 'frow ver rest away. All anyone fuckin' needs is a lit'l bit a patience. We'll 'ave knowledge Iron. As much as we ever did need. I swear it.

Sweetheart is over by the door. He turns back to them.

Sweetheart 'E's back. The geezer. Back where 'e was. Corridor. Same place no kid. Books an' all. Christ 'e's a big bastard. Jacket like before. 'E's lookin' schraight at me. Ain' movin'. 'E must a' come back no question. 'E's seen me see. 'Oi Mister where was you, wot 'appened? Teabreak was it? We're over 'ere, we ain' moved 'ave we? (*watching*) 'E's comin' vis way. Honest. Fuckin' is. On 'is way. 'E is honest. Our direction. Oh this is it. This is it. Lovely. Thass the one. Mister keep on comin'. Slo-owly. Slo-owly now. Don' stop nah. Keep it comin'. There yer go. Yer lookin' good son. Lookin' beautiful from where I'm standin'. Ea-asy nah. Keep right on comin'. Oh you are lookin' beautiful. Aincher though? Beautiful. Ainch yoo jus' beautiful.

And then, somewhere a long way away a bell goes for the end of school, a long, long note. We hear the sound of doors being slammed and, far-away all the racket of school breaking up. Sweetheart, his face quite without expression, turns back into the room and crosses back to sit at his desk. The class sit in silence, with nothing more to say. Slow fade.